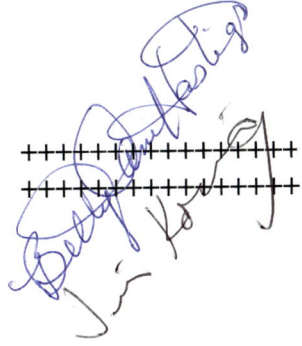

HAVING FUN ON THE DESERT

by
Jim Koning
and
Betty Ann Hastings

Foreword by Terry Gerber

Cover photo by Jamie M. Colee
Illustrations by Jim Koning

2016

++
++

++
++

Copyright © 2016 by Jim Koning and Betty Ann Hastings

Having Fun on the Desert, its authors and any other persons associated directly or indirectly with this book assume no responsibility for any misinterpretation of contents, accidents, losses, or injury by any group or individual using this book.

++
++

DEDICATION

This book is dedicated to all the firemen, police officers, and members of rescue teams who tirelessly work to save others and often sacrifice their own lives in so doing, with a special dedication and tribute to the Granite Mountain Hotshot Firefighters from Prescott Arizona, nineteen of who lost their lives on June 28, 2013, fighting the Yarnell Fire.

Jim Koning wrote this as he was watching the procession escorting the bodies to Prescott.

> I watched as the procession went by again,
> I stood and honored the valiant men.
> Twenty men, the crew held in all.
> For nineteen, it was their last call.
> If you'd ask them now, to a man they'd say,
> "Please don't cry. No tears, no way.
> We knew of the danger that lurked that day,
> Had to answer the call and go anyway.
> People were in danger, we were needed,
> So the fire alarm we heeded.
> Now we look down and it makes our hearts swell,
> To see us honored and thought of so well.
> To see so many who we never knew,
> Mourn our loss and say, "thank you".
> That's all the thanks we'll ever need,
> To be appreciated for our good deed.
> To be remembered for what we do,
> Now, in turn, we say, 'thank you' ".

ACKNOWLEDGEMENTS

We would like to thank the many people who shared their knowledge, answered our questions, and otherwise helped us with this book.

A special thanks to Rusty Hastings for sharing eighty plus years of gathered information from desert living, his patience for hanging out and waiting many long hours while we worked on our manuscript, and adding tremendously to the book.

Thanks also to our proof readers, Susie (Sudsy) Elfritz, Diane and Cherry Waters, Jaime Colee, Linda Waters, and Rusty Hastings.

We are indebted to Joshua Hastings, mechanic and lifelong desert resident, Mike (Shaggy) Lett, backcountry hiking guide, Sean Sheehan, backcountry hiking guide and rescue worker, Frank Meyerholz, hiking guide, and Terry Gerber, Interpretive Ranger at Lake Pleasant Regional Park.

Members of the Maricopa County Sheriff's Department, Phoenix and Peoria Police Departments, Phoenix, Morristown, and Peoria (especially Tim Eiden) Fire Departments were very cooperative in answering our many questions, as were the Phoenix and Deer Valley Offices of the Bureau of Land Management.

We are grateful to our numerous friends in the Maricopa Lapidary Society and the Wickenburg Gem and Mineral Club, many of whom are not with us anymore, for their guidance and tutoring from our early childhood into our adult years.

Foreword

Starting back in the early 1970's, I spent time as a young buck growing up in the Arizona desert. My older brothers and I would venture out into the playground of this desert, of which I had little knowledge at the time. I was lucky to have big brothers who possessed better understanding of the dangers that existed in this beautiful, but unforgiving place. To my benefit, I was a fast learner and thus soaked up knowledge and skills about proper desert travel.

One summer, I was graced by the privilege of working at the Grand Canyon in the Youth Conservation Corps. That was my real hook. I found the outdoors intriguing and wanted to spend my life in those outdoor places, learning to not be afraid, but rather respectful and self-reliant. Through my college studies, I gained an understanding and appreciation for the desert as I focused on wilderness management and outdoor recreation. Some people might dream of becoming a park ranger, but I finally had that opportunity and took hold. The time spent working in a desert park setting has blessed me with a benefit of coming to terms with this wonderful but harsh desert.

The best place I know to learn knowledge of the desert is from the people who spend a significant amount of time in this environment. I encourage you to spend time in these pages of knowledge, which comes from true outdoorsmen, Betty and Rusty Hastings, and Jim Koning. They know the desert well and have experienced many adverse conditions, furnishing you this valuable information.

Desert awareness is an art and a science. After all these years in the desert, I can walk right through a patch of teddy bear cholla and not get one piece stuck on me, although another guy hiking in the same group ends up with several of these menacing pokers stuck to them. I also find I am the only one in the group who thought to bring a comb and pliers to pull out the cholla parts and spines. Desert awareness is truly that: being aware of your surroundings and having the knowledge to avoid negative situations. It also is being prepared for many situations, having the skills and equipment to enhance your odds for getting out of such predicaments you might find yourself in during an adverse incident, stranded problem, or even in a desert survival situation.

The following pages will enlighten you on the issues that can come up in a harsh desert. As you venture through this book, you will also receive tips, knowledge, and ideas for further skill enhancement, hopefully making your desert adventures less stressful. You will learn things, as to watch out where you place your hands and feet in the desert. You will pick up advice in taking care of yourself, taking care of the people in your group, and taking care of your equipment. Advice on planning and knowing local land management laws will help set you up toward your travels. Also, knowledge of desert wildlife and plants is always helpful when venturing into the southwest outdoors.

So enjoy your journey through these very informative tidbits of desert awareness. After reading through these pages, you will have the advantage of knowing what these seasoned ranch hands have found useful in preparing for their desert ventures. I wish you well in your reading and a good stewardship discovery of the Southwest deserts. May your exploring be wise, respectful, and safe.

Terry Gerber

Interpretive Ranger
Lake Pleasant Regional Park
Maricopa County, Arizona

PREFACE

Several times a week on the evening news, one can be assured of seeing a story about disaster on the desert. People suffer all types of mishaps in which they are injured, and all too often, die. Not only have their lives been disrupted, sometimes permanently, but also those of rescuers. The personal financial toll as well as that of the rescuing entity can be devastating.

One evening while watching an especially disturbing disaster report, my brother, Jim, and I realized that there was a great need for the public to be more aware of desert conditions and how to avoid unpleasant experiences. We also knew that aside from newscasters and rescue crews desperately trying to explain things after the fact, there was little to inform people how to avoid desert emergencies and how to cope with them if they occurred.

Having lived in rural Arizona most of our lives, and having spent a lot of time with our gem cutter/prospector parents camping and hunting gemstones in remote areas of the Southwest, we have seen and helped with many emergency situations involving other people and have experienced a few of our own, as well.

As children, our parents taught us about desert survival almost daily, and we received training from some of their friends who were desert survival experts, such as Lee Kelly, a noted teacher of survival skills for private groups, as well as for the U.S. Army.

Some of these individuals contributed a lot to our education, even if we did have to eat grasshoppers and drink from pools of water that were much less than pure in order to pass their courses.

As an adult, Jim was a dispatcher and sometimes firefighter for the local fire department for ten years, during which he took part in many rescues. He also received extensive training in survival in the military.

My husband, Rusty, and I have lived in remote areas of Arizona, such as the bottom of the Grand Canyon and the Arizona Strip, for the past thirty years. We have often lived under mesquite trees and in covered wagons for several years at a time.

While I was wishing someone would write a book to help people safely navigate the desert, Jim suggested that maybe we were qualified to do this ourselves, and if we wanted to see a book with that subject matter be made available to people, maybe we should get it in gear and do it.

So we did. Our book contains information for both the inexperienced and experienced desert dweller or recreator. We have included information to help prepare for and prevent emergency situations from arising. Should an emergency occur, there is information on how to cope with it and perhaps minimize it so that it doesn't become a matter of life or death.

There are many animals and insects on the desert that a person can encounter. Some of these may not be familiar. Perhaps a person has heard of them or encountered them casually, but has not had personal experience with them. We have included information about a lot of the most common species and what to do if they are encountered while on your outing or around your home.

Our book is not intended to be a "desert survival" book as such. It's rather a collection of information and advice to help individuals stay out of desert survival situations. Desert survival situations are dire and not what anyone venturing out on a camping trip or excursion to have fun in the desert wants to, or should, experience. Many, if not most, of these scenarios can be prevented with a little knowledge, foresight and preparation. It's this knowledge that we hope to impart to people who live and recreate in the southwest.

INTRODUCTION

During the past several decades, there has been a huge influx of people into the Southwestern United States. People relocate here for many reasons. Employment opportunities and the climate are two of the biggest factors. Along with new permanent residents, a thriving tourist industry has developed, attracting visitors from all over the world.

Even though the population has more than doubled in the past twenty years, the Southwest is still largely rural and has a lot of open land, such as Bureau of Land Management areas, national forests and monuments, county and state parks, and more. Much of this land is accessible to the public for recreation, prospecting, and other uses. It has become easier for the public to purchase the plentiful number of four wheel drives, quads, dirt bikes, and other toys that have made recreating on the desert more fun than ever and have helped open up areas that were difficult or impossible to reach with former modes of transportation. This has resulted in thousands of people on any given weekend flocking to the desert to enjoy themselves.

Many of these recreators and new residents aren't entirely familiar with how to cope with the unique conditions and harsh climate, both summer and winter, that make the desert different from other places. This often results in finding themselves in difficult situations with resulting problems that people don't understand how to solve because of their lack of experience.

Not just newcomers can find themselves in predicaments on the desert. We have seen experienced outdoorsmen, including ourselves, in tight situations because they have either had an unexpected occurrence or breakdown or have gotten careless and overlooked some precaution that they should have taken or known about. When disasters are reported, it's often stated that, "He was an excellent outdoorsman", "She was an excellent swimmer", "He was an expert equestrian", and so forth.

Emergency situations don't have to lead to disasters with catastrophic results. If a person is prepared and has taken the proper precautions, these situations usually can be resolved in a timelier manner and with a much happier outcome than if a person is totally unprepared. Preparation for a simple desert outing can literally make the difference between life and death if an unpleasant and unexpected event takes place while you are out there.

There are many things a person can do to prepare themselves to meet various emergency events that can take place while on the desert. Each and every one of them will help ensure your safety while on your outing. Being safe is the number one priority when it comes to having fun and arriving home in one piece.

TABLE OF CONTENTS

SECTION I Safety First

	Page
Desert Safety-Starting Out	19
CPR and First Aid	19
Land Use—Know Where to Go	20
Desert Etiquette	22
Have a Plan	28
Preparing Your Vehicle	32
Water	36
Food and Medications	41
Clothing	45
First Aid Kit	47
Pulling it all Together	48
Items to Keep in Your Vehicle Permanently	49
Items to Take on a Day Trip	50

SECTION II Into the Desert

Into the Desert	53

Your Vehicle…………………………………………………	53
Know Yourself………………………………………………	58
Avoid Getting Lost………………………………………...	59
Lost Despite all Your Preparations…………………	64
Vehicle Accidents…………………………………………	65
Dehydration and Hyponatremia……………………	68
Hypothermia………………………………………………	73
Fire……………………………………………………………	76
Flooding…………………………………………………...	85
Sand………………………………………………………...	90
Hiking and Backpacking……………………………...	96
Water Safety……………………………………………...	99
Pets and Animals…………………………………………	102
Firearms……………………………………………………	107
Mining Areas……………………………………………...	111

SECTION III   Desert Animals

Rattlesnakes………………………………………………	123
Tips for Avoiding Rattlesnakes……………………	129
What if I am Bitten by a Rattler…………………	132
Coral Snakes………………………………………………	136

Coral Snake Venom	138
Avoiding Coral Snakes	138
If Bitten by a Coral Snake	139
Scorpions	139
Avoiding Scorpions	144
What to do if Stung by a Scorpion	147
Black Widow Spiders	148
Black Widow Spider Control	151
If Bitten by a Black Widow	151
Arizona Brown and Brown Recluse Spiders	153
Brown Spider Venom	154
Brown Spider Control	155
If Bitten by an Arizona Brown Spider	156
Tarantula Spiders	157
Tarantula Hawks	159
Gila Monsters	160
Gila Monster Venom	162
Myths about Gila Monsters	162
If Bitten by a Gila Monster	163
Other Facts and Information	164
Centipedes	165

Centipede Venom………………………………………………..	166
Avoiding Centipedes…………………………………………….	167
If Bitten by a Centipede………………………………………..	167
Africanized Bees-What They Are…………………………….	168
How They Got Here……………………………………………...	168
When They Reached the United States……………………….	169
How Fast They are Spreading………………………………..	169
What They Look Like…………………………………………..	169
Killer Bee Venom………………………………………………..	170
Avoiding Africanized Bees……………………………………..	170
What to do in the Event of a Bee Attack…………………….	171
Conclusion………………………………………………………..	172

++
++

Photo by Sudsy Elfritz

SECTION I

SAFETY FIRST

++
++

DESERT SAFETY-- STARTING OUT

Safety in the desert begins before you ever leave your home, even for a short trip. People think, "Well, I'm only running out to the lake for a little while," or "We're only going on a little picnic for a few hours." Emergencies can occur, even in a short time.

We own and operate a riding stable on the Arizona desert. Many times, people who are stranded or in need of help see our establishment, which is the only structure for miles around, and come to us for help. Most of these people were only planning a short recreational trip into the desert to have fun for a few hours and didn't bring along provisions that may have been needed, such as spare tires, a jack, a tow chain, enough gasoline, or adequate water. The Boy Scouts have their motto "Be prepared" for a very good reason. If you aren't prepared for the worst, an emergency can land you in trouble. If you're prepared for the worst, an incident that may have been an emergency may turn into just a minor inconvenience or never happen because you have taken pains to circumvent it before the fact.

CPR AND FIRST AID

Before setting out into the desert, you should take a course in first aid and CPR. You may never need to put this knowledge to use, but if you do need it, you will be glad you have it. The wilderness is a lonely place when you're sitting there waiting for help for yourself or an injured person and you don't know what to do. Prompt action is often necessary to save your life or someone else's. If you don't know what to do and do the wrong thing or nothing at all, it could contribute to further injury or even death. If you're sure what action to take, you may save a life (maybe even your own). At the least, it will make a bad or uncomfortable situation better.

Even if you don't usually leave your home, we advocate first aid/CPR courses. You never know when someone will be injured or have a heart attack, a stroke, break a major bone, choke on food, or some other medical emergency will arise, and you'll need to apply first aid or perform CPR until professional help arrives. You can find simple courses by going online or calling your local fire department, hospital, ambulance service, or college to see where these courses are being taught. It's well worth the effort.

LAND USE—KNOW WHERE YOU CAN GO

Before venturing out on your excursion, make sure you know what entity or agency controls the land you're planning to visit. Besides a few types of land, such as Indian reservations and limited acreage regulated by counties, such as county parks, there are essentially three kinds of land in the Southwest: Federal, State and private.

Federal land is controlled and administered by the Federal Government under the Bureau of Land Management (BLM) and is owned by all citizens of the United States. It consists of national parks and monuments, Reclamation land, national forests, wilderness areas, open land, and more. It's generally available free to all of us for recreation and prospecting. Commercial ventures need special permits, and any commercial or other revenues collected for use of the land is used for maintaining it. All Federal land in the United States has basically the same laws and regulations no matter which state you happen to be in because it's controlled by the Federal Government. If you are coming to the Southwest from any state, you can safely assume that the rules here are pretty much the same as where you are from.

State land, however, is much different from Federal land in its rules and regulations. State lands are structured, controlled and administered by each individual state and often are held in trust for beneficiaries and public institutions such as schools, state universities, hospitals, charitable institutions, and prisons, with revenues collected for use of this land going to various beneficiaries. Laws governing and regulating state land can vary widely from one state to another.

Private land is administered by the individuals who own it.

There are rules for the use of each type of land, whether Federal, State, or private. Violations may result in fines, jail sentences and other legal tangles, such as impounded vehicles, weapons, fishing gear, and more. For this reason, you need to be sure of what type of land you'll be using and what the rules are. Check with the branch of the government or persons administering the area you will be visiting.

Maps indicating types of land by section can be obtained from State and Federal agencies, some bookstores, prospecting supply stores, or online. Private owners can be located by checking with the county, a local real estate office, or the internet. Check with private land owners for permission to use or cross their property. Many don't want people on their property and they have posted "No Trespassing" signs. If you don't see "No Trespassing" signs, don't assume that the landowner doesn't care if you use or cross his land. Many times signs have been vandalized or torn down.

There are roads that a person can travel and ones that are off limits. Recent changes in the law have resulted in the mapping of desert roads that have been deemed allowable for travel. Check with the agency governing the land you'll be visiting and get a map. If the road that you want to use isn't shown, it may be against the law to go there. At no time is it permissible to cut across the desert with any type of vehicle, making one's own road or trail.

When you become familiar with existing areas and laws, continue to check with State and Federal agencies to keep abreast of any new regulations, as land use laws can change often.

DESERT ETTIQUETTE

When you're on any land in the desert you're a guest there, even if it's federally controlled and owned by all of us. When you look on a map of the Southwest, you'll see that compared to other terrains the desert is actually a small place. The burgeoning population and encroaching civilization has shrunk it even further. Much of it has been destroyed or damaged by irresponsible visitors.

The desert is a great contradiction in that although it can be very harsh and hardy, it's also fragile. Changes to the environment and even what may seem to be slight damage to the landscape, wildlife, cacti and other vegetation, may have more of an impact than what one would assume. Not only is the landscape unique, there are plants and animals living there that exist nowhere else in the world. When they're gone, there will be no more. It's the responsibility of each individual to conserve and protect the environment for future use for both others and ourselves. State, Federal and County agencies, as well as environmental groups such as the Sierra Club, are all happy to provide guidelines for preserving the environment. Some of these agencies provide workshops on environmental protection that are open to the public.

Although rules and codes of conduct may vary from one type of land to another and be somewhat different according to various controlling agencies, there are some rules when visiting any area that will remain the same. One of the most important is: "Don't litter! If you pack it in, pack it out". It's vital to leave campsites and picnic areas in good condition when you vacate. Cleaning up behind you is more than just preventing the desert from becoming an eyesore. There are a host of substances such as aluminum, plastic, tinfoil, and more that don't biodegrade for years, especially in dry desert environments. Many assume that the few items they're leaving behind won't be noticed, but due to growing population and easier access to remote areas, trash can pile up very quickly. This not only ruins the scenery for all who come after you, but irreparably damages the environment. Some items you may leave behind can be toxic to animals or endanger wildlife living there. For example, animals can get caught in strings, wire, or plastic. They can eat food or other items that make them sick or prove fatal. Even if garbage left behind is safe for eating, wildlife living near campgrounds and places of human habitation can become dependent on human refuse. They can also lose their fear of people. The latter has resulted in attacks on humans by these animals when they see a person, and that individual has nothing for them to eat.

Many householders put food out for wild animals so they can watch them in much the same way that they would watch wild birds at a feeder. Birds are one thing, animals are another.

Recently, it has been in the news that people in certain areas, such as the retirement communities of Sun Cities, Arizona, have been attacked by coyotes and chased by javalinas. In one instance, in a new housing area in greater Phoenix, a coyote got into a house and chased the children. In Cyprus, California, in July 2013, a two year old girl was attacked and dragged by a coyote while visiting her grandmother's grave in Forest Lawn Cemetery. It's not known for sure why animals that usually don't bother humans are now losing their fear and attacking, but it's thought that possibly it's because we're encroaching more and more on their territory. Also, maybe they're getting too used to people feeding them.

Private individuals and clubs, as well as certain government agencies, have spent untold money and man hours cleaning up litter and debris and have hauled trash out of the desert by the truckload. These cleaning expeditions have been very costly in tax dollars and workers' time.

At Lake Pleasant County Park, in central Arizona, for example, paid workers as well as volunteers regularly pick up trash and garbage. Once a year, a National Public Lands Day is held and volunteers clean desert areas, including Lake Pleasant Park. In spite of the constant regular cleanups that are done year round, approximately twenty pickup loads of trash are removed from the Park each time this cleanup is held. During a cleanup at nearby Table Mesa, at least thirty truckloads of trash were removed by the Bureau of Land Management. The area was such a mess that it was closed to motor vehicle traffic for a period of time. Thirty to fifty truckloads of trash and debris are removed each year from the Box Canyon area near Wickenburg, Arizona. When brush and weeds are cleared from the right-of-way of any major highway, the trash exposed often is of staggering proportions despite the "Adopt a Highway" program, in which volunteers periodically clean along the roadside.

Due to rising costs of fuel, fees, and distances to landfills, many people are hauling their garbage to the nearest rural area and throwing it out. As a result, the desert has become a dump with everything from furniture and appliances, to car bodies, tires, and bags of household trash strewn about.

It doesn't take much thought to realize what will happen if this type of behavior continues. So even if it costs a little money, properly dispose of unwanted items and household garbage. Take sacks with you and bag your trash when you go on trips to the desert. If there are dumpsters or garbage cans provided, see that your trash winds up in them. Some people take extra sacks and bags with them, and they pick up trash and debris that others have left and dispose of it appropriately. Most gold prospectors who are metal detecting carry a bag with them for trash such as cans, bottle tops, wire, and other scraps.

Besides keeping clean any area of public land you're using, there are other rules of wilderness etiquette, as well. Cacti and desert flora are protected and should be treated with respect. We have seen many cacti and bushes flattened and ruined from being run over with vehicles, shot full of holes, hacked open to see if there is really water in them, and even uprooted and left to die. Cacti don't just grow up like weeds. Saguaros, for example, take over a hundred years to develop to full maturity.

Destroying cacti can also destroy you. Some of them fight back, particularly saguaros. These cacti can weigh up to four tons. In one instance, a man was shooting at a saguaro at very close range, when a limb fell on him and killed him. Another person was trying to topple one of these giants with his truck. He backed up, took a run toward the cactus and slammed into it. As it fell the top portion backlashed, caved in the canvas top of his vehicle, killing him.

Thorns from the cholla cactus are some of the most painful in existence and some varieties such as the teddy bear, or jumping cholla, are composed of sections which come loose at the slightest disturbance. They're light and can sail through the air, giving the appearance of having been thrown or jumping at a person. If you're walking by or among them and happen to brush lightly against them, or even very near them, an entire section can fly off and stick into you. Once they are in you, they're very difficult to extract. Throwing rocks at jumping cacti, hitting them with sticks, shooting into them, or other methods of destruction are also not good ideas. We have pulled thorns from many people who have run afoul of these cacti from doing some of these things. A few of them wound up in the hospital. All cactus thorns are mildly toxic, and many who have been punctured by large numbers of them get sick from them and can take weeks to heal.

It's against the law to dig up cacti and other plants, even though you may not be destroying them and intend to replant them in your yard. If you want a specimen, contact the agency responsible for the land you plan to take it from and see if there's a way to obtain a permit to do so.

Most varieties of cacti and desert flora can be purchased from nurseries. This probably will not only prove to be less expensive and less trouble than digging them up out of the desert, but the nursery will give you instructions for planting and care of your cactus, tree, or shrub.

A lot of public land is used by ranchers, who have permits to raise and graze cattle and other livestock. They have fences, water holes and tanks, windmills, salt licks, and other supplies and provisions for their animals. None of these or the rancher's livestock should be disturbed.

If you pass through a gate that's closed, it's proper etiquette to close it again. If it's open, it's customary to leave it open. Since a good share of desert land is leased for grazing and livestock, any gate is probably located on a ranch. If you close a gate that's open, you may be closing livestock off from water or feed. If you leave a gate open that you found closed, livestock may escape to an unsafe area, such as an area with access to a highway or other road where they can be killed or maimed by traffic. This could also possibly cause injury or death to people, as well as damaging vehicles and other property.

Without fences, animals not only can get into areas where there may not be adequate water or feed, but the vegetation can possibly harm them. Some plants, such as "loco weed," can injure the brain and/or neurological system and sometimes lead to death. In the best of cases, livestock may wander off onto someone else's land or other land where they shouldn't be, causing the rancher time and money to round them up. There are many reasons for open and closed gates.

It's imperative that watering areas for livestock always be treated with respect. Animals will die quickly without water, particularly during summer, because they need a lot of water in the heat. A horse or cow, for example, will frequently drink up to fifty gallons of water over a twenty-four hour period during the hottest part of the summer, Without water, a cow can survive from two days to a week, depending on the breed. An Angus or Hereford will only last about two days. A cross breed or longhorn can live up to a week, eating cacti for moisture. A horse can survive without water for only two to three days, and if he becomes really dehydrated, he'll suffer extreme stress. Even if he gets rehydrated and survives his ordeal, he'll often suffer mental and/or physical difficulties the rest of his life.

Much too often, people shoot water tanks full of holes and destroy windmills, drying up the supply of water for the livestock and other animals that depend on it. Often, they camp or hunt right by the water, keeping the animals away. It's illegal to camp or hunt within a quarter mile from any water source used for animals, either wild or domestic.

Ranchers check waters as frequently as possible, but their busy schedules and large areas to cover often allow them to get to these places only about every five or six days. Contrary to movies and television shows, ranchers are seldom rich or have much money. A dead cow or bull represents a huge investment. Good horses are valuable assets, and the death of a well-trained horse can be devastating both financially and emotionally.

This isn't a complete list of desert etiquette. A general rule of thumb is to treat the desert with the same respect that you would treat your own home and yard. In effect, public land is your own. You are one of the persons paying taxes and fees that go to the management and upkeep of the land. Disrespect is only going to hurt you and everybody else in the long run.

Destruction of the land has led to the government closing off certain areas to the public, and high fines or jail sentences are imposed if you're caught littering or vandalizing it. Destruction of the land ruins it for everyone's, and your own, future use.

HAVE A PLAN

Before venturing into the desert even for a short time, you need a plan. It doesn't need to be elaborate. This may seem silly and time consuming, but if you travel into the desert a lot you'll eventually wind up running into some type of problem, either your own or you'll find someone else in trouble. Also, as you become used to planning, it will become second nature, and you'll do it without even thinking much about it.

The first thing to do is to let someone reliable know where you're going and when you plan to return. If you aren't back at the appointed time or shortly thereafter, your backup person will know that you have run into trouble and will be able to either look for you themselves or alert authorities to begin a search party. If you're going to be gone for a longer period of time, such as several days, it's best to designate times that you'll check in with your backup person. In the desert, this simple step can and has made the difference between life and death.

Jim worked with the local fire department for almost ten years and was involved in a lot of rescues of stranded and lost people. Most of the people having difficulties hadn't performed the simple step of letting someone know where they were and when they were expected to return. Had they done so, many would not have needed the fire rescue because their backup would have already been there when they didn't check in. By the time anyone realized that anything was the matter, some of these people were already in pretty bad shape because of exposure to the elements. Some persons were even found dead. Although it is extreme, people have been known to die within three to five hours when temperatures reach over a hundred fifteen degrees.

When telling your backup where you're headed, you should be as specific as possible. Provide a map if necessary. Don't take it for granted that just because you mention a certain broad area, your potential rescuers will know exactly where to look. Provide as much information and as many details as possible about the vicinity you plan to visit, and stay within that area. The desert can swallow you and make you difficult to spot. There have been times that rescue parties have passed within a few feet of a person because that person was either unconscious or too weak to call out.

Some of the best advice we know is to not to go out alone, even though you may have alerted a backup as to your whereabouts and return time. If you suffer a mishap, such as a vehicle breakdown, get stuck in sand, sprain or break a limb, get snake bitten, have a heart attack, sudden illness or accident, you'll have difficulty dealing with it alone. Many people have come up against such emergencies and barely, or not, survived.

For example, a well-known survivalist who usually went out alone, fell and broke his leg just a mile or two from his vehicle. His cell phone had no reception. His backup alerted the authorities, who several days later found him still alive but dehydrated, hungry, and in pain. Had he had someone with him, it would have saved him a lot of discomfort. Had he not told his backup where and when to look for him, he most likely would have died.

Fortunately, modern technology has provided help for a lot of emergency situations. However, electronic devices should never be completely depended upon, as they tend to fail at very inconvenient times. Always have a backup when using them for emergencies.

Your cell phone can be your best friend if you're in trouble and need help. However, you must have a charged battery.

Smart phones have an emergency locating device that's always on. If you have an older phone, you have to activate the GPS locater yourself. If you're making a regular call, you must have reception to use either kind of phone.

When you dial 911, however, even if you have no reception, your call will be picked up by satellite, and you'll be connected to emergency services if you're using a smart phone or one with a power booster. Your position can be pinpointed to within a few feet if you have a strong signal. If your location is remote, and if you don't have a strong signal, your position can't be located as precisely. The dispatcher may have to ask specific questions as to your whereabouts. He may need descriptions of landmarks, mountains, rivers and so forth. You can also ask emergency services to get in contact with your backup, because they'll know where you are.

In-vehicle security, communications, and diagnostics systems, such as Ford's Sync and OnStar by General Motors, are great to have installed in your vehicle, as models are available that run off satellite and don't depend on wireless phone service. You're never out of range of communication with emergency help. If you have an accident, you'll automatically be connected with a live operator. You'll also be able to dial a live operator at any time. You don't have to be in your vehicle to do this, as a free OnStar app is available to download onto your phone, and Sync can be contacted by phone. If you don't already have one of these systems, it's possible to have one installed, depending on the model and age of your vehicle.

The value of these systems can be illustrated by the following event: Four people were about twenty miles into the desert in a four wheel drive car on a day in late spring when the temperature was 118 degrees. One of the tires blew out. The spare tire wouldn't dislodge from beneath the car. The owner of the vehicle called OnStar, and rescue was on the way. The alternative to this comfort and convenience could have been a lot grimmer.

In another instance, two young women were stranded when they discovered they had locked their keys in their truck while on their outing to a remote area. The situation quickly got ugly when they panicked and each began blaming the other for their plight. They began fighting, hitting each other, and pulling out hair. When Betty and her husband happened upon them, they were exhausted, angry, scratched to pieces, and had large hunks of hair missing. They said that they had been best friends for years, but now they never wanted to see each other again. They began pelting the windshield with rocks and hitting it with tree limbs, trying to break it in hopes of being able to reach the keys inside.

This incident occurred only about three miles off the main highway on a dirt road. Cell phone service was available, but neither had a phone with them. Had they had one of the aforementioned emergency systems and a cell phone, they could have easily called for help, and their vehicle could have been unlocked remotely, saving their friendship, their dignity and some of their hair.

Betty's husband pointed out that they had just loaded their quad onto the hauler, they had gasoline in it and the quad keys on their person. He advised them to ride their quad to where they could call for help.

If you spend a lot of time recreating in remote areas, it might be worth your while to invest in a SPOT satellite GPS messenger device. This is a small unit (some models are only 2x3 inches) that's capable of tracking you wherever you go. There's a map, and a person can get on a home computer and track your progress if you're on a long back-country journey. SPOT has an "I'm OK" button you can press to notify the folks back home that you're just fine. There's also an SOS button if you encounter an emergency situation. If you press it, your GPS co-ordinates will automatically be sent to a search and rescue center, which will go into action on your behalf immediately. As of this writing, there is a new model SPOT which will plug into your smart phone, enabling you to send e-mails and texts whether or not you have a wireless signal. In addition, SPOT has a satellite phone available.

One might think a SPOT device would be very expensive, but it is actually moderately priced, and when you think of what it can do for you, it's really very cheap. SPOT products can be purchased at outdoor supply stores or online.

PREPARING YOUR VEHICLE

It's of primary importance that your vehicle is in good running condition before setting out anywhere, especially into the desert.

There are few things as aggravating or potentially hazardous as finding yourself stranded in the wilderness because your vehicle has suffered a minor malfunction and you neglected to bring the basic equipment needed to repair the damage. Checking your vehicle completely before you go can seem like a hassle, but it's nothing compared to the hassle of finding yourself stranded because you didn't take proper precautions.

One of the biggest mistakes people make is failing to check the fluids in their vehicles. Not only do you need to fill your radiator, but you need to see that motor oil, oil in the differential, and transmission fluid levels are full. Everyone knows to take extra drinking water while in the desert, but people don't always think of extra water for their radiator. Take extra with you or even extra radiator coolant. Make sure your gas tank is full. You'll want to take an extra can of gas or two with you. Take extra motor oil and transmission fluid.

Fan belts, radiator, heater, and power steering hoses should be replaced every three years in dry desert climate.

Check your tires. Be certain your tires and your spare are inflated properly. Sometimes it's a good idea to bring two spares if you're going into especially remote or rugged country, if you're going to camp for a few days, or do a lot of four wheeling. A portable air compressor that plugs into a cigarette lighter is a must. Take a jack, a lug wrench for removing tires, and anything else you may need to change a tire.

More frequently than one would suppose, we encounter people who have neglected these basic precautions. Many people struggle into our facility asking for our help because they've neglected to bring a jack or spare tire or have run out of gas. We also have seen them walking along the road, footsore, and often thirsty and hungry, sometimes wet and cold, or too hot. We keep extra supplies for those who reach our riding stables and need to use our phone to call for help or ask to borrow our tools and even, on occasion, our tires. One unfortunate man spent the night in his car in front of our stable because he had a flat tire and no jack. The temperature was 27 degrees and he had no jacket or blankets. We brought him inside, warmed him up by our fire, gave him breakfast, and loaned him a jack. He realized how lucky he was to have had his mishap near our place, and he expressed his gratitude a few days later by bringing us a really nice jack for a present.

A high lift (handy man) jack is good to bring with you. Although this type of jack can be used on many SUVs and four wheel drive vehicles, it can't always be used on many newer models of passenger vehicles because often the bumpers aren't made to hold the weight of a car or to fit a jack. If it can be used on your vehicle, it's better to have it along than not. It has a broad base, and is less apt to push into sand if you're trying to change your tire in a sandy place. It goes lower than a lot of other jacks, and you can get it under a bumper more easily than a regular jack. It can also be raised higher. Handy man jacks come in 48 and 60 inch lengths.

Even if your vehicle isn't one that will accommodate a high lift jack, it's still good to have one along because it can double for other purposes. For example, it can be used as a ram.

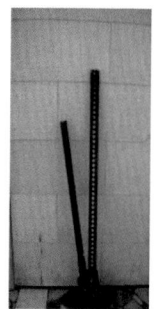

High lift jack

We came across a man who had slidden off a steep, loose gravel road. The front of his vehicle had lodged against a large boulder and was hooked to it. He was unable to back up. We took a high lift jack, put the base against the boulder, put the hook on the side of the bumper, and pushed the truck away from the rock, freeing it so he could back up.

This jack can also be used as a come-along by putting a chain through the top loop, fastening it to the stuck vehicle, attaching another chain to the lift hook and anchoring that to something solid. Then, just jack your vehicle forward. Use chain for this operation, not rope or tow strap. Regular rope can break, and tow strap can stretch.

With a little imagination (which you will probably have if you are desperate and in a pinch), a high lift jack can be used for many things that don't even pertain to vehicle emergencies. Ranchers are never without them. For example, they can be used to lift out fence posts, stretch wire, and many other things that we haven't even heard about. You shouldn't be out in the desert removing fence posts, but you never know what emergency you may come up against, and you'll need all the help you can get. They don't call these "handy man" jacks for nothing.

Be careful when using a high lift. Keep a firm grip on the handle, especially when you have it jacked up high. The weight of the vehicle or object you have on the jack can easily cause you to lose your grip, and the handle can hit you in the face or head. If you're listening and paying attention, you can

High lift being used a come-along

hear and feel when the jack locks into place. If it isn't locked into place, the weight of the vehicle will cause the jack to slip down to the next notch or further, causing the handle to fly up, rendering a gaping hole somewhere in your flesh, or knocking you unconscious if it should hit you. Serious injury and death have sometimes occurred from accidents with handy man jacks.

One of the best things you can have with you at all times is a pair of jumper cables. These may not only help you, but may help others, as well. So many people have come to our stable needing jumper cables that we keep a spare pair on hand to loan. Next to help with flat tires, jumper cables are probably the most common need of the people seeking help that we encounter.

Dirt roads are harder on vehicles than paved roads. Breakdowns occur more frequently than when you're driving on pavement. You should take a good tool kit for basic repairs, and also take a few spare parts, such as fan belts and fuses.

Know how to use your equipment and how to do minor repairs as needed. Because dirt roads tend to shake things apart, it's good to have tie wire in your tool kit to wire together bumpers, mufflers, tail pipes, and other parts of your vehicle that may loosen.

It's easy to get stuck in sand on the desert, so bring a come-along, tow strap or chain, as well as a shovel.

Each person, their situation, and vehicle are different. We may not have covered every special need for each person. Give your particular situation some thought, and remember the basics. Many a person has been stranded in an uncomfortable situation for lack of a half-inch wrench, or because they didn't know how to change a flat tire or fan belt.

WATER

Water is the single most important thing a person can have in the desert. If you take nothing else with you, take water. This cannot be emphasized too heavily. You can't survive long without water, and it's scarce on deserts.

Dehydration is the number one enemy when you're out in the elements. As has been mentioned earlier, people have been known to die from dehydration within three hours if temperatures reach 115 degrees or over, and these temperatures aren't uncommon in the summer in the Southwest.

There is on record the case of an older man and two young men, ages 20 and 21, who were on a military range near Yuma,

Arizona, stealing brass shells. They were going to sell them as scrap metal. The temperature was 120 degrees that day.

Patrolling military police saw them, and the older man fled, leaving the two younger men. Not seeing the two who were left behind, the police gave chase and caught the older man, who admitted after about an hour that he had left the others in the desert. The military went back out to the area and found the two young men dead from dehydration. This all took place within a three hour period.

In another instance, a jet pilot ejected over the Arizona desert in the Eagle Tail Mountains just north of Yuma. He survived the crash in apparently good condition, but was found dead the next day. From examination of the body, proximity to the airplane, and the way the man was walking, it was estimated that he had died of exposure within four hours after he ejected.

The two examples just cited are extreme but not necessarily uncommon. People have been known to survive longer than the above mentioned men without water in the desert and have been rescued up to three days or more later. But these are people who didn't lose their heads, and although they hadn't brought enough water or prepared for emergencies, knew how to take measures to ensure their safety and prolong their life.

Never rely on finding your own water once you get out into the countryside. Don't rely on using any of the methods in desert survival manuals to produce water to drink, as some of these methods won't work and at best provide very little water.

Likewise, there is no cactus that can be hacked open to find a pool of water inside. While some cacti have moist interiors, they don't contain enough moisture to appreciably rehydrate a person, most of them don't taste very good, and some will give you diarrhea, dehydrating you further. However, the fruit of some cacti, particularly prickly pear, is very nourishing and juicy and will help stave off dehydration. But to take advantage of this fruit, you'll need to time your emergency to happen from mid to late summer when the fruit is in season.

Never drink the water from your radiator. It usually contains antifreeze and other chemicals that will poison you.

Water purification tablets are an excellent item for you to have with you if you become stranded and it becomes necessary to drink from a lake, water hole, stock tank, spring, stream, or seep that you may be able to find. It's wise not to drink from any source of water you may find on the desert without purifying it, because it may contain contaminants such as dead animals that you don't see that may be submerged beneath the water. There may be bacteria or minerals that may make you sick. You can contract giardia, dysentery, typhoid, anthrax, and a host of other illnesses carried by animals, or even people. A lot of these illnesses will cause upset stomach, vomiting, and diarrhea, further dehydrating you.

Minerals such as arsenic or sulfur in the water may make you ill. Purification tablets won't help. If water tastes bitter, don't drink it, even if you have purified it, because there will probably be enough arsenic or sulfur in it to upset your stomach.

You may boil water for about 1-3 minutes to purify it. This step will destroy bacteria, but boiling may not be an option because you may not have time to build a fire, wood may be scarce, or you may not have a proper container. You may not have much water to begin with, and boiling for any length of time will evaporate much of your liquid.

Although many people go out in the heat of the summer, most take desert outings and hikes when the temperature is between

80 and 100 degrees. The average person exposed to the elements at these temperatures needs a minimum of eight ounces of water every half hour. If they're exerting themselves by walking during the heat of the day, they'll need at least eight ounces of water every twenty minutes. At night, when temperatures are cooler and the humidity rises, a person doesn't dehydrate as fast. They should have about eight ounces of water every forty-five minutes.

All this translates to each individual needing at least three gallons of water for a twenty-four hour period. This may seem like a lot of water, but don't underestimate how fast you can become dangerously dehydrated, even if temperatures are not extreme. The reason for this can be attributed to the very dry desert air.

How easily a person can become dehydrated can be seen by turning on the evening news anywhere in the Southwest and noting the frequency of incidents in which hikers and others recreating on the desert need rescue because of dehydration in temperatures that are not particularly high. In fact, whatever the reason for a person needing rescue on the desert, they're dehydrated to some degree. There are no exceptions.

During the weekend of March 11-13, 2011, five rescues of hikers were performed by the Phoenix Fire Department in the parks and mountains surrounding the city. The high temperature of the day didn't exceed 85 degrees. One of the rescued individuals had passed out, injuring his knee when he fell. He not only had to be given intravenous fluids for dehydration and to bring his core temperature down, but had to be treated for the knee injury as well. Every one of the rescued people were dehydrated, potentially leading to a fatality during a simple hike in a park.

During the winter months when it's much cooler, the need for water isn't as great as during the summer. However, it may surprise you to learn that you can dehydrate even in cool and cold weather. It will take longer for it to happen, but it will happen if you aren't properly hydrated. The desert air can be so dry (4-6 % humidity) that your body can dehydrate before you realize what is happening. You will need at least eight ounces of water every 45 minutes to an hour during cooler weather. During periods of higher humidity, you won't need as much water.

It's a myth that all liquid consumed will keep a person hydrated. Soda pop, coffee, tea, and other beverages containing caffeine cause dehydration. Alcohol will also dehydrate you. This is because both of these substances are mildly toxic and the body tries to excrete them by making the cells produce water to flush them out.

Gatorade, Powerade, and other sports drinks are good because they replace electrolytes that water alone won't replace. But these beverages are sugary, and sugar, although it will provide a little temporary energy, will cause you to feel thirsty.

Fruit juices, likewise, can be good because they contain a certain amount of food value and the sugar provides energy. However, keep in mind that they may make you feel thirsty.

Some experts feel that pedialite is a better choice than sports drinks, as there is no sugar in it. It's used by many search and rescue teams. But when it all comes down to it, there's no substitute for good old H_2O.

A final point about water: even if you're not planning to leave the highway or town, you should have a supply of water with you. If you break down, you may wait for some time for help. Distances in the Southwest can be great and tow service to rural areas, between towns, or even within a town, can take a long time. If the day is hot, you could end up really wishing you had brought water with you. The infirm, young children, and the elderly can have medical issues.

During one hot summer, an elderly couple broke down in their pickup truck in an area that's sparsely populated but still inside the city limits of a large city. The temperature was 109 degrees and the truck's engine was inoperable, so running the air conditioner wasn't possible. There were no trees for shade. The couple called a tow truck using their cell phone, but it took over an hour and a half for help to arrive. Fortunately, they had emergency water with them. Without this, conditions could have been very uncomfortable and even dangerous for the elderly couple, especially as the man had previously suffered heat stroke and had a low heat tolerance.

When the tow truck driver finally arrived, he offered them bottles of water. He told them that he was used to bringing water to stranded people, as most didn't think to carry it for emergencies. Many Highway Patrol and Sheriff's Department officers in the Southwest also carry bottled water for anyone they find stranded along the highway.

FOOD AND MEDICATIONS

Besides water, you need food. While a person may be able to survive relatively easily off the land for a period of time in other areas, it's difficult to do so on Southwestern deserts. Game is scarce and difficult to catch, and edible vegetation is sparse and seasonal. If you have an emergency and have to be out there for even a short time, you're going to get very hungry.

Some people like to gather their own wood for cook fires. If this is your plan, you'll need to check with authorities for rules on wood gathering in the area in which you plan to camp. Laws differ from place to place and according to the type of land you'll be staying on. One option is to bring your own wood with you for cooking and campfires. You'll need to check with authorities to see if it's possible to have a fire where you'll be going, as fires are prohibited in certain areas, and there are usually seasonal fire bans in most parts of the desert and forests. This goes for charcoal fires as well as for wood. Except possibly during times of extreme danger of fires, small gas burning stoves are usually acceptable even when there's a fire ban.

Many people prefer to use charcoal to cook their meals and take their own camp stoves or charcoal grills with them. If this is your plan, don't forget to bring extra charcoal and/or fuel for your stove and lighter fluid for the charcoal if you aren't using the easy ignite type.

Never attempt to start any fire using gasoline or diesel fluid. People know this, but they do it anyway, and the dangers this poses cannot be emphasized too heavily. Never pour lighter fluid or gasoline onto a fire that is already ignited.

Matches are essential on all outings, whether or not a person plans to cook meals or have a campfire. The best type to include in your supply kit are "strike anywhere" wooden matches. Special waterproof containers for matches can be purchased at outdoor centers.

You will need to take one or more ice coolers for perishable items such as milk, meat, eggs and produce. Carefully examine your coolers to make sure the lids fit tightly and there are no cracks in them that would allow cold air to escape.

You will need adequate ice in your cooler. Due to the heat and dryness of the desert, it will melt more quickly than in other climates. Take more than you think you'll need, especially if the weather is hot. If you are opening your cooler frequently, such as to get cold drinks from it, the ice will melt more rapidly. You might want to take an extra cooler just for the drinks and keep the food in its own cooler where it will remain cold and fresh. Some people like to include block ice as well as cubed, as the block lasts longer and also helps the cubed not to melt as quickly as it would ordinarily. Some people take an extra cooler full of ice that they don't open except for replenishing the other coolers. If you put a small block of dry ice in your coolers, it will make your ice last longer.

Cooler water may be contaminated with bacteria and should not be consumed except as a last resort. However, it may be used as wash water or to soak cloths to wrap around your neck or put on your head to keep you cool. You may also immerse your forearm in it to cool your blood. You can pour it into your drink cooler, as the water will keep the drinks colder than just the ice. But if you chose to do this, remember that the ice in the drink cooler will melt more rapidly because of the warmer temperature of the water.

You should also take along canned goods, prepackaged foods and meals, and other items that don't need refrigeration. This can eliminate a lot of coolers and ice that might take up space in your vehicle. You'll be glad to have canned meats, canned milk and other similar items if something should happen to delay your return to civilization or some catastrophe should befall your coolers.

Secure your coolers and supplies well, as more than one person has lost a cooler out of the back of a pickup or open jeep.

For planned meals, dried and dehydrated foods are great. But if you're running low on water, you may not want to use it to rehydrate food.

It's important to include snacks in your food box, because eating lightly from time to time can help replace energy and electrolytes that will be lost as you engage in your activities. You'll also need them if you want to hike away from your campsite or if you find that you have to walk a long distance, such as if you are stranded or your vehicle breaks down. Often while having fun on an excursion or if it's hot, a person either forgets about eating or simply doesn't feel like eating. But if you have healthy snacks with you, it can be easier to remember to nibble on them from time to time.

Snacks to take with you should include lightly salted items such as nuts, chips, pretzels, dried or fresh fruit, granola bars, trail mixes, and similar items. A lot of snacks are high in sodium and can make you feel thirsty, so use these in conjunction with a lot of water. Fresh fruits such as oranges, peaches, plums, and apples will help keep you hydrated. Bananas and dried apricots are loaded with potassium, and lightly salted snacks such as nuts, chips, and pretzels will help replace lost sodium. Granola bars and trail mixes will help provide energy and help replace electrolytes. All fruits have sugar and will help keep up your energy levels during hikes and during emergencies.

Plan to accommodate any of your medical conditions that may necessitate a special diet. Don't forget to include any medications you may be taking. Take enough medication to last for a few extra days just in case an emergency strands you. Too often, while watching the evening news, you hear of someone who has gone missing and the news anchor says, "This is of special concern because this person needs medication to survive and is without it." You don't want to be this person.

CLOTHING

In addition to food and water, you're going to need adequate and appropriate clothing and other protection for your body.

Moisturizer, sunscreen, or sun block on the desert is a must, even in winter. This is especially true if you're usually inside. You should also have a protective moisturizer such as Carmex or ChapStick to protect your lips and a good lotion for your hands. The elements are very harsh on your skin. If you're going to use sunglasses, get polarized ones that will filter out UV rays.

You should also have a hat, and wear it summer and winter. Hats not only shade you from the sun, but will slow down dehydration all year round. A lot of moisture is lost from your body through your head by perspiration and rapid evaporation. A hat will help keep the moisture in your body and shade your face, as well as keep your head cool in summer and warm in winter. Broad brims will shade more of your face and the back of your neck than a narrow brim or baseball type hat. Hats of straw, palm frond, or cloth are best for summer, as they are more ventilated and allow air to circulate more freely. Heavier hats, such as felt and canvas are better during winter. Lighter colors reflect the sun and are best for hot weather, while the darker colors are better for winter, as they absorb and retain more heat.

Many people think that when they pull off their shirts and other clothing and wear shorts and outfits of minimal covering, that they are going to be cooler. This is true when the weather is not severely hot. In extreme heat, however, the opposite is true. You may initially feel cooler, but during temperatures of 95 degrees or more, light, protective clothing is better than bare skin. Exposing bare skin to hot sunlight raises your core temperature, causing rapid evaporation and dehydration. A person doesn't need to bundle up, but light, even gauzy, fabric breaks the sun's rays. It holds moisture from perspiration close to the body while allowing the air to flow through the material. This slows down evaporation and therefore, dehydration.

You can confirm this by touching your body under your clothing, and then touch your skin where the sun is directly hitting. Feel the difference in the temperature of your skin. Excellent clothing made of special fabrics for hot weather wear can be found at outdoor and sports shops. Cotton is great for hot weather wear, as it allows air to circulate through to the body.

Footgear is a very important consideration when you're outdoors. You'll need comfortable boots or shoes suited to your activity. We've seen women show up for horseback rides in high heels. We've seen them trying to walk and hike in them, also. People have been known to embark on desert hikes wearing sandals, flip-flops, or cloth tennis shoes. Women have been seen trying to hike down the trails in the Grand Canyon wearing everything from high heels to flip-flops. None of these are appropriate. There are sharp rocks, dirt, gravel, twigs, branches, cactus thorns, and all kinds of objects lurking in the desert that are hostile to the human foot. The key to having your feet in good condition is protection. Hiking boots and sturdy shoes are best for desert wear. Cowboy boots are all right, but they aren't suited for walking very far.

Socks are a must. It's surprising how many people have gone on hikes without them. While you may be able to go without socks in the city, once you get into the desert on rough ground, you're doing a whole different type of walking. Socks protect your feet from a lot of irritants such as sand, pebbles, and dirt that will sift into your shoes. Your feet won't blister as easily with socks. Socks also absorb sweat and are much more comfortable than trying to go without them. If you are wearing a boot or high top hiking shoe, wear a high top crew sock. If you use a sock that doesn't cover your ankle and leg up to the top of your shoe or boot, your footgear will chafe your skin and can cause discomfort, blisters, or irritation, which could easily become infected. It's best to select a sock of cotton or cotton blend.

Gloves are another handy item to bring along. You'll need them in order to avoid ants, scorpions, and other insects when you gather firewood, turn over, or pick up rocks. They are protection from thorns and slivers and will prevent blisters if you're digging. The best gloves are leather or leather palmed. Cloth or gardening gloves aren't substantial enough and will easily be torn or punctured by thorns and cacti. Handling cacti is never a good idea, but especially do not handle them with gloves. Thorns tend to stick in gloves, especially if they're small or fine. They will be impossible to remove.

Although the desert is mild in temperature during the winter, it can fall below freezing. Breezes and winds can be extremely chilling. You will need adequate sweaters, jackets and even rainwear. A blanket, even in summer, might come in handy, as night temperatures often fall 30-50 degrees cooler than day temperatures. If daytime temperatures have been 105 degrees, you can feel chilly enough to need a blanket if it is in the 70's during the night.

FIRST AID KIT

First aid kits are many and varied. They can be as small as a box you hold in your hand to the size of a rucksack. The size and type of first aid kit you take with you is a personal choice, but it should include several sizes of adhesive bandages such as Band-Aids, some specialized ones like butterfly bandages, and ones that fit over the ends of fingers. Ace bandages and a large triangular bandage should be included.

There should be gauze bandages of different sizes and a roll of adhesive tape for securing these. You'll need blunt tweezers and scissors. Trauma scissors are best. You should include antiseptic cream for open wounds, burn ointment, an antiseptic ointment or spray, moleskin for blisters, rubbing alcohol, hand sanitizing wipes, cotton swabs such as Q-tips, cotton balls, a minor pain reliever such as aspirin, ibuprofen, or similar medication of your choice, fever thermometer and disposable medical gloves.

You can customize your first aid kit with items you'll need that are not included when you buy the kit, such as flashlights or thermal blankets. Don't forget any prescription medication that you may need. Be sure to include extra for emergencies.

An important item to customize your first aid kit to the southwest is duct tape. There is almost nothing on the desert that doesn't prick, puncture, stick, or otherwise bite. Sooner or later, you or someone with you is going to run afoul of very fine thorns which are in some cacti, such as prickly pear, pencil chollas, and other vegetation. They are almost flesh colored, difficult to see, and if you get one you get a million. They're next to impossible to extract with tweezers and are extremely irritating. They are also mildly toxic and can make a person itch and swell in the area where they are lodged. Your first impulse will be to try to rub them out of you, but don't do this because they break off and are still in you. The best way to get them out is to cover them with duct tape and then rapidly remove the tape. Most of the thorns will adhere to the tape and you will be free of them. You may have to repeat the process a few times, but it works better than any other method that we know.

PULLING IT ALL TOGETHER

The things we discussed in the preceding section may seem overwhelming, but as we've mentioned before, after you've gone into the desert a few times, everything will seem easier and soon you'll be including all needed supplies and items without thinking much, if anything, about it.

A lot of necessary items don't need to be loaded and unloaded constantly, but should be permanently stored in your vehicle. That way, you'll always have them on hand and won't have as much to remember each time you go somewhere. And again, the alternative to not having them when you need them can be much more unpleasant than taking the trouble to organize them and have them on hand.

Each person has individual needs, so the following list is just a suggested guide. You will want to tailor it to your particular situation.

ITEMS TO KEEP IN YOUR VEHICLE PERMANENTLY

This may sound like a lot to carry around with you all the time, but you can break down anywhere at any time or run across someone in need of help. This may not be a complete list of what some people will need, but it's intended as a start.

    Tool kit

        Jack (you may also want to carry a handy man)
            Board or block to stabilize the jack

            Lug wrench
            Spare tire
            Fix-a-flat
            Portable air compressor that runs off cigarette
                lighter or other source
            Extra parts (simple things like a fan belt, fuses,
                and hose clamps)

Extra length of gas hose
Extra fluids (brake and transmission fluids, radiator
 coolant, motor oil)
Water for radiator
Jumper cables
First aid kit

ITEMS TO TAKE ON A DAY TRIP

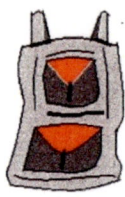

Two gallons of water per person (this
 includes extra for each person)
Water for any pets
Other beverages as desired
Food and ice cooler
Hatchet and/or hand saw
Matches and other fire sources such as
Aiming Flames or cigarette lighters.
Charged cell phones, GPS, SPOT or other
 electronic devices and car charger

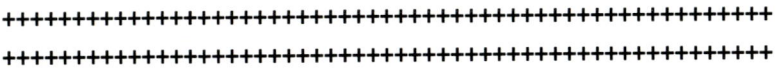

Section II

INTO THE DESERT

INTO THE DESERT

You are ready for your desert adventure. You should now have with you all the necessary food, water and equipment that you need to enjoy yourself.

YOUR VEHICLE

You need to know your vehicle well enough to know if it's suited to go where you are going and that it's capable of doing what you expect it to do or what it may become necessary for it to do.

Many people assume that if you're going to travel off road, you will need a four wheel drive vehicle. Four wheel drives are helpful for off-highway traveling but are not always necessary. There are many dirt and gravel roads that a passenger car can easily navigate. However, before doing so, you may need to do a little checking, and you'll need to be careful traveling.

A good way to begin checking roads is to call whatever agency is responsible for their upkeep, such as the state or county where you'll be traveling. If they can't help you, they can often give suggestions and direct you to someone who can.

One of the easiest ways to tell if your car can go over a road is to ask a local authority, such as a law official or person living in the area. Most people living in outlying areas are friendly and helpful and will do their best to give you good advice. Not only do they not want to see anyone stuck or in trouble, they don't want to see anyone on their doorstep at midnight begging for help to get out of some bad situation.

Another way to tell if your car will navigate the road is simply to look at the road carefully. If it appears to be well maintained and graded, it probably is. If it becomes rough or you are in doubt, you can always turn around and come back. Be observant, and if you come upon an area where the road looks bad, if it's washed out or really sandy, if there are big rocks, or other obstructions such as brush or vegetation that your vehicle might not clear, it's best to turn around.

In addition to turning around when the road may become too rough for your vehicle, it's imperative not to take a short cut that you aren't familiar with or drive your vehicle off a good road onto one that is very primitive. An elderly couple traveling through north central Arizona took a wrong turn and decided to take a shortcut to get back on the right road. The shortcut looked simple on their map, but it was a road that wasn't maintained and was very seldom used.

At first the going was good, but after a few miles the road got a lot rougher. Rather than turn around, they continued on in their two wheel drive car. They came to a stretch that had large rocks, deep ruts, and brush. Trying to continue, the car became disabled, and they were unable to proceed further.

Stranded, they waited with the vehicle, hoping a search party would be launched and help would arrive.

In fact, a search party had been launched, but they didn't know where to look because they didn't know that the couple had tried to take a shortcut. The man and his wife continued to wait for help that didn't arrive. After a few days, the wife died. The husband decided to walk for help and was eventually spotted by searchers. He was taken to a hospital where he spent several days recovering from his ordeal.

Use caution when straddling brush with a low clearance vehicle. Brush traps blowing dirt and sand, and there's often a dirt mound under and around it which can cause you to high center your car. Sand and brush may be covering large rocks, and boulders and you won't know they're there until it is too late and you have perhaps badly damaged your vehicle by tearing out important parts such as oil pans, transmission and gas lines, electrical cables, and more.

Be especially careful that you don't run over cacti because the thorns from many kinds will work into your tires. They won't work themselves out because they have barbs similar to an arrow or fish hook and won't pull out easily. These barbs travel forward because they are smooth going in. You may not notice the damage immediately, but somewhere down the road, and maybe at a very inconvenient place, you may experience flat tires or leaks.

If you're traveling in a four wheel drive, the same principles apply as for a passenger car. The only difference is that a four wheel drive can navigate rougher roads than a car, and it has a higher clearance. Don't make the mistake of thinking that because you have a four wheel drive you can go "anywhere". Those television commercials are misleading! Four wheel drives have their limitations and can get stuck or damaged just the same as any other vehicle.

One case that springs to mind is that of a dehydrated and sunburned young woman who arrived at our riding stable in the heat of an August morning with a man on a quad who had rescued her. She and three other women had been traveling in a four wheel drive pickup truck and discovered that they were on the wrong road. Consulting their map, they found that the road they wanted to be on ran parallel to the one they were already on, and it was only about a mile from them. They decided to cut across country to it.

They set off across rugged, impassable terrain and soon became mired in a sandy wash. Unable to go further, they panicked, revved the engine and spun the wheels until they were buried up to the axle. They had no shovels to dig out of their situation and no food. There was nothing to drink but a small amount of water from melted ice in the bottom of their cooler. There was no cell phone reception. All of them were dressed in sandals and flip flops, shorts, and halter tops.

Leaving the other three women with the vehicle, the lady managed to get back to the road and catch a ride with the man on the quad.

In another case, a man was going up a mountain to the Four Peaks amethyst mine east of Phoenix. There was an area that was really steep where most people parked their vehicles and walked. There were a lot of trees, and pine needles on the ground were several inches deep. The man had a four wheel drive that he assumed would go "anywhere". He didn't take into account that other vehicles had parked and not gone further or that pine needles are slippery and it would be impossible to get traction. His jeep began to slide and eventually wound up so far down the mountain that it couldn't be retrieved. Fortunately, he was able to walk the fifteen miles to the nearest help. The last anyone knew, the jeep was still on the mountain.

The speed your vehicle can travel over rough terrain is probably one of the most misunderstood things in terms of knowing what your four wheel drive is capable of doing. Commercials on TV feature professional drivers operating four wheel drive trucks, jeeps, and ATVs going at break-neck speed over rough terrain, through water and up and down mountains so steep that a mountain goat would have a problem going there. People see these misleading commercials and think they can drive this way because their vehicle is meant to perform under these conditions.

While it's true that your four wheel drive will go more places and take more punishment and abuse than a two wheel drive passenger car, it's still just a vehicle and will break down and wear out quickly if treated the way advertisements insinuate it can be utilized. Driving fast over bumpy desert terrain can result in stone bruised and ruined tires, loose nuts and bolts, broken welds, ruined shock absorbers and springs, broken windows and windshields from rocks flying up, just to mention a few things. The vehicle will fall apart, its life will be shortened, and maybe your own life as well.

In time, your vehicle will rattle apart over dirt roads, even under the best of circumstances. One rural mailman who makes a thirty seven mile loop six days a week over a rough, but well-traveled gravel road, goes through at least one set of tires a year. He has two four wheel drive trucks because one is usually in the garage being repaired. He said the most common problem he encounters is that the front end assembly is constantly being rattled apart. He has to have the front end aligned often. He has had door hinges rattle loose and the door on the driver's side fall off. The tail gate on his late model four wheel drive pickup has fallen off twice. He doesn't use it very often. Keep in mind that this is a very careful driver and has been negotiating desert roads all his life.

A rancher we know wore out a brand new horse trailer in just one year hauling horses and hay over dirt roads once or twice a week. His ranch was only about six miles from the highway.

Finally, "Speed kills" is true in the desert as well as on paved highways. Our interviews with police and fire departments reveal that the most common cause of accidents and fatalities in off road accidents is speed. Very often, alcohol is involved. It is far easier to lose control of a vehicle on rough terrain than on pavement. At the scene of one accident on a dirt road popular with recreators near our stables, a policeman told us that his department is called out to that area at least once each weekend for a speed caused accident, which often involves serious injuries or death.

KNOW YOURSELF

After making sure your vehicle is in good shape and has what it needs, you have to make sure you are in condition for what you're going to do, or what you may have to do. You'll need to take into account what kind of physical shape you're in and if you can walk the distance you intend to go. Realize that if you're hiking out you're going to have to hike back. If you're traveling downhill, remember that coming back will be harder. You should also know your heat tolerance.

Not knowing what you're capable of doing is one of the major mistakes people make while on desert excursions. Betty and her husband rescued one such lady in the Grand Canyon. She had assumed that she could come from a sedentary life in town and hike in three digit temperatures through rugged terrain to Supai village at the bottom and back in one day, a total distance of sixteen miles round trip. She had fallen behind her party, who went on without her. She became lost and wandered into a seldom traveled side canyon. When Betty and her husband found her, she was nauseous, disoriented, and incoherent.

On June 2, 2013, when temperatures were approaching 105 degrees, a group of three young men attempted a ten mile hike into the White Tank Mountains, a short distance from Phoenix. About four hours into the hike, one of them, just twenty one years old, became disoriented and weak, stating that his legs wouldn't move. He tried to continue, but in spite of help from his companions, collapsed. Attempts to revive him using CPR failed. Help was called via cell phone, and the young man was pronounced dead at the scene.

Knowing what you are capable of doing can be tricky, and even trained professionals can make mistakes in this area. A desert-wise prospector and lapidary who had lived in Arizona and hunted for gemstones for many years made the mistake of wanting to hunt gems in the heat of the summer in one of the hottest areas in the southwest. He should have known better, but he had never had difficulty with heat in the past and didn't take his advancing years into account. Because he was elderly, and because of the time of year, our dad advised him against going, but he insisted. Our dad, not wanting him out alone, took Jim and accompanied him.

They arrived at the location of the agate field, got out of their truck, and began hunting gemstones. The temperature was at least 118-120 degrees.

About fifteen or twenty minutes into the hunt, the elderly prospector was overcome with heat. He began running around, screaming, and babbling. Our dad had walked away and was out of earshot over the hill hunting gems. Jim grabbed the old man, sat him down on a rock under a tree, put a cool, wet, cloth on his head, and tried to get him to drink water. He had to force water down him, as the man was out of his head. He kept jumping up and running around and continued screaming and babbling. He refused to keep the wet cloth on his head and was incapable of listening or understanding. Our dad finally heard the noise, returned, and helped Jim put the man into the truck. He was too weak by then to do much struggling, but he continued to scream and yell all the way home and had to be taken to the doctor, where he was treated for heat exhaustion and dehydration.

AVOID GETTING LOST

It's easy for anyone to get turned around, confused, or lost in remote areas.

As has been mentioned earlier, the cell phone, GPS, OnStar,

SPOT, and similar devices have made it less likely that a person will get lost than in previous times, and if they do, technology has lessened the seriousness of it. However, you may find yourself without one of these aids or with a failed system. Things can always go wrong with technology, no matter how wonderful it is, so you need a backup plan.

The best backup plan is to be desert-wise. It's really unpleasant to be lost in the wilderness, and if you have to be rescued it will cost the agencies who search for you time and expense, will cost you time, and may wind up costing you money, as well. It's much better if you don't get lost in the first place. There are many tips to help keep you oriented.

There are two types of situations that make it difficult to locate a person. The first is when someone needs rescued but they can't tell rescuers exactly where they are. They can retrace their steps, but they weren't paying attention to mileage, landmarks, names of roads, and so forth. The second is when the person doesn't know where they are and has become so confused that they can't find their way back to civilization. With adequate preparation, you can lessen your chances of finding yourself in either of these situations.

Although you're going to have a map with you and you have plotted your course, it can be difficult and complicated to pinpoint just where you are. Dispatchers claim that over half of people in need of rescue don't know exactly where they are, and even when they know, they often can't give directions how to reach them.

Aside from maps and GPS, the best way to keep from getting lost or turned around is to pay close attention to where you're going. Roads often look different coming back than they did going out. Turn around every now and then and look behind you to familiarize yourself with how the terrain will appear when returning. Notice mountains, hills, cacti, odd rocks or formations, forks in the road, ranches, buildings, windmills, or corrals that can be used as landmarks. Take note of distances between them, especially known ones that have a name. Note your mileage and keep track of how far from the main road you've traveled. Know which direction you're going. A compass will tell you which way you're headed.

If you break down or run into trouble, and you have taken the above precautions, you'll have a very good idea of where you are. You'll be able to tell a dispatcher, for example, "I'm in Trilby Wash about three miles north of the Red Picacho." The closer you can get the rescuers to you, and the faster they can find you, the better off you'll be.

Another good reason for taking note of distances between landmarks is that this knowledge can help you find your way back should you become confused. For example, if you remember that if you're three miles from a certain landmark, and you go back more than three miles without having seen that landmark, you're going in the wrong direction.

When Jim was dispatching for the fire department, a man who broke down walked in looking for help. All he knew was that his car had broken down in a wash somewhere off the main dirt road. He estimated the distance to be about three miles away. He hadn't noticed any details on his way out and was unsure of how to get back to his car. It took rescuers a long time and a lot of wandering back and forth and up and down several washes before the vehicle was found.

When the car was finally located, it was six miles away in a wash that was well marked on maps and on a well-known road. If he had consulted a map and noticed his odometer, he could have simply said he had high centered his car six miles from town and the final two miles were up San Domingo Wash.

In another instance, a man had become lost in the mountains on his quad and called 911 from his cell phone asking to be rescued. He didn't have the slightest idea of his location. He couldn't tell how far from the highway he was, where he left the main road, or anything pertinent to his situation except that he was lost somewhere in the mountains between the two towns of Wickenburg and Wittmann. This constituted a twenty mile stretch of many square miles and innumerable roads. The area was very brushy and mountainous, which would make it difficult to spot him from the ground and almost impossible from the air. He had no water, no food, his phone was cutting in and out and often he had no reception. Night was approaching, and he was beginning to panic.

Rescuers could not pinpoint where the man was by using his cell phone locator because his reception was too spotty. Fortunately, the County Sheriff's Department was able to locate him by helicopter. He was airlifted out. He was suffering from dehydration and fatigue. He was less than three miles away from the main highway. He had no survival skills and didn't realize that all he had to do was climb up on one of the hills and he would be able to see traffic. Because it was not very hot, he could have walked to help.

Later, in spite of several attempts, he was unable to find his way back to his quad. As far as anyone knows, it's still out there. All this could have been avoided had he noticed where he was going and the number of miles he had traveled from a point such as the main highway or a specific town. A good GPS would have been invaluable.

It's very important to know how to talk to the dispatcher at an emergency number when you call for help. Dispatchers don't necessarily know your area or the questions to ask. They often will ask for the nearest intersection, not understanding that there may not be one for miles, or if there is an intersection, that in a rural area the roads may have no names. If there are names, they may not be posted. This is where your map may come in handy. If the roads have names but are not posted, they could be on the map.

One rescue team had a difficult time locating an eighty year old man who had wrecked on his quad. The dispatcher asked him what the nearest intersection was, and he told her but neglected to mention that he was eight miles from there. The dispatcher told the rescuers he was near the intersection he had stated, but of course, when they got there, he wasn't there. His cell phone was either turned off or not working, so he couldn't be tracked that way. The rescue team searched a three mile radius, finding nothing.

It was finally discovered when the man managed to call in again, that he was "down the road a ways" from the intersection, but he had no idea how far. His cell phone cut out again before he could be tracked through it. Fortunately, he did know which road he was on, and rescuers found him by following it until they located him. The man was badly injured. He suffered a broken leg, head injuries, multiple scrapes and contusions, and was dehydrated. Had he been better able to communicate his geographical position, he could have been rescued much sooner, saving himself several hours of pain and agony.

Many people find themselves in need of rescue because they're lost or turned around. Some of these folks are embarrassed to admit that they need help. They don't call 911 until the situation turns more serious. By this time, they are in bad shape and often relatives and friends have become really stressed and worried about them. Cases have even occurred where people finally called for help, but hid from the rescuers and tried to follow them back.

Don't ever be afraid to contact the authorities for help. That's what they're there for. That's their job. They want to help and that's why they're working where they're working. They see many lost people and won't judge you. They're just glad when they find you alive, or find you in time to prevent something really serious from happening to you.

LOST DESPITE ALL YOUR PREPARATION

There are occasions where you may become lost despite all your preparations. For example, maybe you've parked your vehicle, hiked a distance out of sight from it and find that in spite of noticing landmarks and trying to gage direction and distance, you're still turned around. Maybe you're in an area where you know your cell phone won't work and you have inadvertently left your compass or GPS on the seat of your vehicle.

If you become lost, you're going to suddenly feel lonelier and more isolated than you have ever felt before, and you'll probably also feel rising panic. Keep your head and your sense of humor and realize that you're not the first person ever be lost. Most lost people are found.

Once you have fought down your panic, find a place to sit, either in the sun if it's cool, or under a bush or tree if it's hot. Take your time to look over the landscape. If you've been watching landmarks, you should see something sooner or later that you recognize. It may be helpful if you're sitting on a higher place where you can see for some distance. If you've unsuccessfully been trying to get your cell phone to work and are now sitting in a higher place, remember that reception may be better here.

Don't wander around. You'll expend energy and may use food and water that you'll need later. If you're walking around and are already lost, you may compound the problem by wandering even further from where you want to be or may go in circles.

Stay as near as possible to your vehicle, as it's more easily spotted than you'll be and will probably be found before you will. Vehicles are larger than you are, often are bright colored, and can be spotted a lot easier and from a further distance than a person. They're also usually on a road and more out in the open than you may be if you leave them.

If you don't see any landmark you recognize or don't get a sense of where your vehicle is, just stay put. Your backup person will launch a search party when you don't check in or show up. Let some time go by, and when you think the search party is underway and near where you are, it's time to begin signaling. This is the time to send up your flares or light a signal fire. If you've failed to take the proper precautions of arranging your backup plans, there is a high probability that you will die. Most people found dead on the desert have failed to carry out the precautions that we have outlined.

VEHICLE ACCIDENTS

Because most off road accidents are speed related, drive sensibly. Driving on dirt or gravel roads is different than on highways, and it can be dangerous unless you know road conditions and your vehicle's capabilities.

If you have an accident, the first thing to do is contact help. Tell emergency personnel where you are, if you can, and what your injuries are, if you know. While you're waiting for help to arrive, minimize your movements. If you can move safely, and it's hot, you'll want to find shade or a more comfortable place to wait.

If you have no one with you or were unable to contact help, you'll be glad that you've notified a backup. If you haven't arranged for a backup, it can go very badly for you at this time and even be a life or death situation.

The importance of knowing how to drive off road is illustrated by an incident which involved two ladies who were in a quad accident in the Vulture Mountains near Morristown. They thought their ATV was capable of ascending a very steep mountain without a trail to the top. The ladies were both heavy and were riding double.

About halfway up the mountain, the quad flipped over backward because of the weight of the riders and the steepness. It rolled over them, injuring both. The quad ended up almost at the bottom of the hill. The ladies sustained a broken leg, wrist, sprained ankle, abrasions, and other lacerations that rendered them unable to climb back down. They were able to call 911 using their cell phone. They didn't know exactly where they were, and it took about an hour for rescuers to locate them. Once they were located, it was found that the mountain was very difficult to climb and too steep to rescue the ladies in a normal manner. Rescue crews had to climb back down the mountain and send for litter baskets, ropes and other mountain rescue gear.

The temperature was 118 degrees. Rescuers were in a hurry to get the injured women to safety and neglected themselves in their urgency. Because of the difficulty of the rescue, the exertion level was very high, resulting in one paramedic and one fireman being overcome with heat. The paramedic was becoming incoherent and had to be hospitalized. The sheriff's vehicle and the ambulance both got stuck in the sand. Besides endangering their own lives, these ladies had put their rescuers in harm's way.

Many off road accidents involve children and teenagers. In February, 2015, The U.S. Consumer Product Safety Commission, an independent government agency, released a report stating that 3,023 children under the age of 16 have been killed on ATVs nationwide between 1982 and 2013. Of those killed, 1,303 were under the age of 12.

By 2014, forty-four states had passed ATV safety legislation. These laws vary widely from state to state, so you need to check before operating an ATV yourself or allowing your children to do so.

It's never safe to allow a child under 16 to operate an adult ATV. They haven't developed the coordination or judgment to competently handle these machines.

One of the accidents that we saw was when a nine year old crashed a Rhino. He was thrown out of the seat, and it rolled over him severely damaging his ankle and leg.

Even when children aren't fatally injured, they often have physical problems that can last for years or be permanent. An eleven year old that we know, who was not wearing a helmet, crashed a dirt bike and sustained a concussion and fractured skull. For about thirty six hours he hovered between life and death. Three years later, he hadn't yet fully recovered and was still suffering dizziness, loss of balance and coordination, a speech impediment, and headaches.

There is a high accident rate among teens who drive out to desert areas to recreate. Many of these children are having parties, drinking, driving recklessly, screaming at the top of their lungs as they ride on the hoods and tops of their cars. Some are shooting firearms.

Not only have we seen the desert crawling with these kids, but we have seen them crawling out of the desert. We have had some of the lucky ones, bruised, bleeding, frightened, and awaiting police officers and their parents after having made phone calls from our riding stable. We've had unbelieving, irate and upset parents yelling, crying, frightened, disciplining these children and trying to sort out what exactly went wrong.

We've seen unlucky teens being air lifted to hospitals or zipped into body bags and put into coroner's trucks. One senior "ditch day" a sixteen year old boy was killed and his girlfriend critically injured while drag racing on the road near our stable. The boy collided with an oncoming pickup truck, killing a father and his two daughters.

In another instance, five girls had to be rescued from their truck when they went through a guard rail on a bridge while drag racing. After the horror and pain of being trapped for an extended period of time while dangling over the water in the demolished truck, several of the girls had to be flown to nearby hospitals. The rescue took hours and no doubt also took a great emotional toll as well as a physical one on both teens and parents. Situations like this are also especially traumatic and dangerous for rescuers.

DEHYDRATION AND HYPONATREMIA

If you take an adequate amount of water and other drinks with you and drink them regularly, you probably won't become dehydrated. However, if you find yourself without water or having not consumed enough, you'll become dehydrated and may suffer heat exhaustion or heat stroke. Special care should be taken to protect infants, children, the elderly, and people with certain medical conditions, as these individuals tend to be more susceptible to heat than most people.

Animals seem to fare better in extreme temperatures than

people, but even they can have problems, especially if they aren't used to being outside a lot.

Dehydration most commonly occurs when temperatures are high, although a person can become dehydrated even during the winter. Dehydration depends more on humidity than temperature. The drier the air, the faster you dehydrate. The air is typically driest on deserts during the summer months, and this is why more people dehydrate at that time.

In the summer, daytime temperatures on the desert often exceed 110 degrees. It's unadvisable to be outdoors for a prolonged period of time when temperatures are much over 100 degrees. The cutoff for safety is probably at about 105 degrees for most people. However, this is relative to your tolerance to heat, your age, and your physical condition.

For example, in September 2011, two young men were hiking in South Mountain Park, near Phoenix. They became dehydrated and had to be rescued. One man didn't survive. The high temperature for the day: 99 degrees.

At best, when you're outdoors in hot weather, you'll be uncomfortable. At worst, you'll die. The Arizona Department of Health states that over 1,500 people have died of heat related causes in Arizona between 2000 and 2012. Many of these deaths occurred among those who were "used to high temperatures," went out for a jog, hike, or short walk, were overcome by heat and experienced physical difficulties that lead to death.

Dehydration occurs when you don't have enough moisture in your system to keep you cool and sustain proper bodily functions. This can occur before you realize it or feel it. This is why you need to drink whether or not you're thirsty.

It's a myth that thirst always accompanies dehydration. In the summer, this is probably going to be the case. But in the winter when temperatures are cooler, you may not feel thirsty and you can become dehydrated without suspecting it's happening.

Conversely, just because you may be thirsty doesn't always mean you're dehydrated. If you're talking or breathing through your mouth, your mouth rapidly dries out, making you feel like you need to drink. The rest of your body may not necessarily be dry.

The temperature of water and any other beverage you may be ingesting is important. It's okay to drink cold beverages if your body temperature isn't hotter than normal. When you're exerting yourself in hot weather, however, your body temperature rises slightly, and it's not good to quickly drink anything ice cold because it can shock your system and cause you to become sick and vomit. This will dehydrate you further. Cool or tepid liquids are best at this time. A person should drink them slowly, even holding them in the mouth for a few seconds before swallowing.

In extreme cases, drinking cold beverages rapidly when you are overheated can lead to death. It happens more often than what one would think, and there is no way of knowing when it will take place.

Our daughter-in-law's neighbor was working on a roof on a hot summer day. He came down, went into his house, slammed a cold beer, and came back outside. He dropped dead when he started up the ladder to go back onto the roof.

There are certain symptoms of dehydration that you can be alert to both in yourself and in others. The first sign is that a person will begin to look red and flushed, especially in their face. This can mean that they don't have enough moisture or that they have been exerting themselves too much for the temperature. In either case, it indicates that their core temperature is rising. The flushed look occurs because the capillaries just under the skin open, and blood flows to the surface in an attempt to cool the body by radiation, much like the radiator in a car.

If you're by yourself, this is difficult to notice. Sometimes you can feel you're flushed and hot, but that may be only because the sun is beating down on you, and you're not actually dehydrated yet. Now is the time to sit down, preferably in a shady spot if there is one available. Drink a few swallows of cool (not iced) water. This will help cool your core temperature. If you have an abundance of water with you, dampen a handkerchief or your shirt, and place it on your forehead. This will help cool the blood, thus cooling your core temperature. This is a very important step. It's "nipping things in the bud." The subsequent stages of dehydration become more and more difficult to reverse.

If you don't catch this early stage of dehydration and remedy it, the next thing that will happen is that you'll turn pale. This is because the capillaries, being unable to cool you by radiation, are getting hotter. Consequently, they close down in an attempt to force the blood into the bigger internal vessels, where they might have a chance of cooling. But because your core temperature is rising, your blood doesn't cool in this fashion. You'll begin to feel light headed and dizzy because some of the blood flow to your brain has been cut off. You need to sit down in as cool a place as possible, sip (don't glug) cool or tepid water, and keep something cool and wet on your head. This will not stop you from getting worse right away. You are going into heat exhaustion. You will probably become nauseated and begin vomiting, which will dehydrate you even further. Keep sipping water, and stay cool and quiet. You should eventually begin to get better, but it will take several hours. You need to get to medical help as soon as possible.

If you don't begin reversing your condition at this time, you'll become disoriented, hallucinate, and probably become disagreeable and irrational. At this stage, you're going into heat stroke and may discard clothing, run, and panic. You may lapse into unconsciousness. In any case, if no one is with you, or if you don't have help, you'll become unconscious. Without medical attention, you'll die.

Your core temperature is probably 104 degrees or hotter at this point. Keep quiet, sip water and cool off with a wet cloth on the head or all over the body if possible. Don't use cold water, as it will shock the system. Get help as quickly as possible.

If a person reaches this stage, they may not survive. If they do, the convalescence is lengthy, and permanent brain damage can occur. It's vital not to let a person's condition reach this stage.

After all the discussion about getting enough water, we're now going to tell you that it's possible to get too much water. Getting too much water is rare, but it can result in a condition called hyponatremia, sometimes referred to as "water intoxication".

Hyponatremia is a dilution of sodium and other electrolytes in the body. Drinking too much water without replacing electrolytes dilutes them, especially sodium.

When a person's sodium level becomes too low, hyponatremia sets in. The early warning signs can be subtle and may be similar to dehydration and include nausea, vomiting, headache, fatigue, loss of appetite, muscle weakness, muscle cramps, disorientation, slurred speech, and confusion. Urination may be abnormally frequent, and the urine will be clear.

Compounding the problem, the patient often assumes he is dehydrated and wants to drink even more water. This may result in seizures, coma, or death.

Under normal conditions, a person won't experience hyponatremia, and water is the best thing to drink. However, if you're overexerting or if you are sweating profusely, water alone won't replace electrolytes. This is the reason for taking sports drinks or pedialite with you.

Also, it's important to eat a little from time to time because food has electrolytes. This is one of the reasons it's essential to include lightly salted snacks such as chips and peanuts. Many people like to include salt tablets in their supplies, but if you take these, exercise caution and take them only as recommended. Too much of a good thing can turn into a bad thing.

If you or anyone with you begins experiencing symptoms of hyponatremia, the first thing to do is try to replace any electrolytes, especially sodium, that you may have lost. Begin drinking sports drinks or pedialite and eating salty snacks. Seek medical attention as soon as possible.

HYPOTHERMIA

Hypothermia is a condition in which core temperature drops below the required temperature for normal bodily functions. Most often, it occurs in freezing colder climates, during blizzards, and when hikers become stuck on snow covered mountains. But hypothermia can also happen in the desert.

Although overnight desert temperatures can fall well below freezing, it may surprise you to learn that hypothermia can occur at temperatures of 60 degrees Fahrenheit.

Desert temperatures in the summer can differ 30-50 degrees between day and night. Daytime highs may be 80 degrees and lows may be between 50-60 degrees or cooler. This isn't very cool, but due to the difference in temperature, your body is going to feel like it's a lot colder. You can stand extremes of outside temperature, but your core, or internal, temperature is very sensitive and even if it varies a degree or two, it can make a difference.

For example, your normal body temperature is about 98.6, and if you run a fever of 101 degrees, your core temperature has changed less than three degrees, but you certainly know you are running a fever. If you have been out in the heat all day, your core temperature will be somewhat raised. If you're not wearing a light covering and exerting yourself to maintain bodily heat, and the temperature falls to 60 degrees, your core temperature will drop below 98.6 and you'll be really cold and can develop hypothermia. This happens only during prolonged exposure. The length of the exposure depends on the person's tolerance and sensitivity to temperature. For example, an elderly person with a slower metabolism will normally become cold faster than a young person.

The first symptoms of mild hypothermia may be vague, and the patient may experience a feeling of being chilled, begin shivering, and have rapid breathing and heartbeat. If this isn't reversed by methods such as putting on warmer clothing, getting under blankets, exercising vigorously, and drinking warm or hot fluids, symptoms will continue to become worse, and the person will go into moderate hypothermia.

During moderate hypothermia, muscles will contract further, and shivering will become more violent, making the patient somewhat uncoordinated. They will feel literally "chilled to the bone." Movements will slow and become labored. Exercising will become more difficult, and the person may stumble.

Although the victim may appear alert, confusion will set in because small blood vessels will contract, cutting blood flow and oxygen to the brain. The vessels will continue to contract, trying to force the blood inside the body to warm it, resulting in the victim becoming very pale. Lips, fingers, ears, nose, and toes may become blue because the contracted vessels shut off blood and oxygen from these small extremities.

At this point, reversing the situation becomes more urgent, but will also be more difficult and take a longer period of time.

The methods of reversing the patient's condition are the same as in mild hypothermia, but an external heat source, such as getting indoors, becomes necessary. If this isn't possible, build a fire, and put the victim inside a sleeping bag or under blankets with you. At this stage, blankets alone won't suffice, as the body isn't generating enough heat to warm the air cavity between the body and the covers.

If this condition isn't reversed, the person will go into severe hypothermia. If it becomes apparent that moderate hypothermia isn't going to be able to be reversed, medical help should be sought immediately. The victim will experience difficulty speaking and sluggish thinking, such as wanting to go to sleep. They may suffer amnesia, extreme loss of coordination, including loss of ability to use hands and fingers and ability to walk. Metabolic processes will shut down, and all exposed skin will be blue and puffy. The patient will also exhibit incoherent and irrational behavior and may begin taking their clothes off, exposing themselves even further to the cold. They may even try to dig a hole or burrow under objects to keep warm. Pulse and respiration rates will significantly decrease, and there will be rapid heartbeat. Major organs will begin to fail, and clinical death will occur. That is to say, heartbeat and breathing will stop, but there will still be measurable brain waves for a short time. The colder it is, the longer the brain will stay alive, but at this time the patient will probably not be able to be resuscitated.

FIRE

Before planning to build a fire, check with authorities to find out if you can have a fire where you're going. During the hot, dry, months there are usually fire bans. Some places, such as selected high wilderness areas, don't allow fires at any time because of environmental concerns such as the possibility of denuding a sparsely vegetated area, which when decayed would provide needed nutrients to the soil. Also, wood ashes contain lye, which when scattered can ruin certain types of ground covers. Even though fires may be allowed, there are rules that must be followed in building them. Some areas require use of a fire pan or fire cloth when building fires. Because of concerns such as the possibility of introducing foreign species of insects to an area, some places don't allow you to bring your own wood, especially if you're coming from over fifty miles. Your local fire department, the Bureau of Land Management, state, and county offices can answer questions you may have about fires.

Some agencies, such as the Bureau of Land Management, have guidelines and classes for building safe fires that will protect both you and the environment. For example, the BLM has suggestions for fire prevention that you may not have considered, such as the advisability of parking in areas devoid of vegetation. If your vehicle is hot, direct contact or sparks from your catalytic converter can ignite brush. Also, they suggest that you ensure that spark arrestor devices are in place when operating off-highway vehicles, chainsaws, or any other equipment that may produce sparks. Complete fire safety codes compiled by BLM and other entities may be obtained from them or viewed online.

You will need to exercise extreme caution when building fires on the desert. Because of the dry conditions and unpredictable winds, fires easily can get out of control, and once they do, they are very difficult to extinguish.

Should a fire that you set get out of control, the results can be devastating. The remoteness of some of the back country often makes it difficult to reach the area and a lot of precious time is lost before firefighting crews are able to get to the location.

Once crews arrive, there are almost always other problems to solve in fighting the fire. Sometimes the terrain is so rough they can't reach the burning area. In the summer, when most fires occur, crews are battling not only the heat from the fire, but the heat of the desert. The remote location often makes it difficult to reach fire fighters with things they need, such as food and liquid. Slurry bombers may have to fly a great distance because of the scarcity of airports. Water must be hauled for miles to battle the fire, and this isn't always an option.

For example, a brush fire on the Hassayampa River, in Arizona, burned about three acres. Had it been more accessible, it would have destroyed only about half an acre. This fire was not a remote one. It was only about six miles from the nearest fire department and about a third of a mile from the highway. The river was running, and quicksand made it difficult to cross. The brush and vegetation was so thick that it was almost impossible to reach the blaze, and it was thought for a time that a water carrying helicopter would have to be called. In a more remote area, this brush fire would have caused far more damage.

Even though many wildfires causing the greatest attention have been in forested areas, there are plenty of blazes on the desert that have destroyed thousands of acres, burned and threatened homes, buildings and animals, as well as ruined a lot of desert landscape and wildlife habitat.

There have been times in recent years that it seems the entire desert is ablaze. Even in a season with normal rainfall, several fires are usually burning at one time. Many are started by lightning, but it has been documented by the Bureau of Land Management that 68% of fires on public land are human caused and 32% are caused by lightening. The four largest known fires in Arizona were proven to have been started by humans.

In 2005, there were close to two dozen fires, both forest and desert, raging at one time in the state of Arizona, and in 2010, in California, there were over 2,000 fires burning all at once. In 2011, the largest fire in Arizona to that date was unwittingly set by two campers, who mistakenly assumed that their campfire had been completely extinguished.

In view of the above statistics, we cannot emphasize strongly enough, or too often, the need for caution in building fires on deserts or in any other area.

There are times, such as under windy or extremely dry conditions, that it's advisable not to build a fire at all. The wind can carry sparks a great distance, and it dries the air and vegetation. This makes it extremely easy for a fire to start from sparks.

In 2002, when a stranded motorist built a signal fire, strong winds suddenly came up and scattered sparks that resulted in a blaze that burned 2,000 acres in just a few hours. It became known as the Chediski Fire. It took a month to get it under control. By this time, it had combined with the human caused Rodeo Fire, destroyed over 400 homes, caused the evacuation of several towns, destroyed a vast amount of wildlife and animal habitat, killed both wild and domestic animals, and burned over 400,000 acres. All of this made it one of the worst fires in Arizona history.

It isn't always the fire that you have ignited on purpose that can cause damage but also the fire that you aren't aware that you are setting. Fires are set by carelessly discarded cigarettes and matches, unattended or partially extinguished campfires, sparks from backfiring cars, parked vehicles with hot engines or exhaust pipes touching dry brush, controlled burns that blaze out control, and many other types of accidents.

Even innocent actions like leaving glass bottles of water, sun tea, or other liquid where the sun can shine through them have had very unpleasant consequences. This is rare, but it happens. The liquid in the bottle concentrates the sun's rays into a focal point that becomes very hot, much like setting a fire with a magnifying glass. Our mother almost set our home on fire by placing a jar of sun tea on the wood stand of an evaporative cooler. Fortunately, the smoke was seen before the fire ignited into a full blaze. A restaurant and gas station burned to the ground from a jar of sun tea left near combustible items. At least one brush fire was started along the highway from a discarded water bottle still containing liquid. By the time it was extinguished, several acres had been burned.

Although most brush fires in the desert burn only a few acres, some of them destroy large areas, homes, and cost lives. One of the deadliest, most disastrous of these to date has been the Yarnell Hill fire on the high desert near Yarnell, Arizona. By the time it was under control, it had burned 8,400 acres and 129 buildings. It also killed 19 members of a 20 man hotshot team, resulting in the highest death toll from any wildfire in the country since the 1933 Griffith Park fire, which killed 29 firefighters.

A few other large brush fires during recent years were the Cave Creek Complex fire in 2005, that destroyed 243,950 acres. The Delta, Utah blaze in 2012, burned almost 17,000 acres, and the Chariot Fire, which started on the desert near Julian, California in June, 2013, burned into the forest, destroying over 7,000 acres

Once you determine that it's safe to build a fire, you need to know that there are three main components to having a fire: building the fire, maintaining and keeping it from spreading, and extinguishing it completely.

There are basically two types of fires you may need to build. The most common is a campfire for cooking, warming or just enjoying. The other is a signal fire if you are lost or injured and wanting your position to be located.

Your campfire shouldn't be a bonfire because they're dangerous. The bigger the fire, the greater the chance of sparks getting blown onto dry vegetation and spreading out of control and the greater the danger of damaging the environment. The BLM recommends that no limbs larger than a person's wrist be used. You can easily keep warm and cook adequately with fires of this size.

Although a fire may be made using dead wood from the desert, it's best to purchase and bring your wood with you if you're allowed to do so in the area you'll be visiting. Dead wood on the desert is beneficial to the environment, as it decays and provides enrichment of the soil and provides habitats for certain insects and animals.

In many areas where people have camped, there may be little or no wood available. Even in the best of cases, wood is limited on the desert, and it doesn't take many folks starting campfires to denude an area. If you have your own wood with you, you won't be disappointed at not finding any around your campsite, and you will have helped the environment.

Your first step in building a campfire should be to clear brush and dry vegetation for an area of at least thirty feet. This needs to be done even if there is already a fire ring there.

The second step is to gather stones to make a fire ring if there isn't already one in place. This should be a ring about three feet in diameter consisting of rocks about the size of your head. Some campgrounds and areas require you to use a grill or fireplace that's already there.

It's best to use a fire pan or fire cloth underneath your fire. These can be purchased at outdoor and sports shops. They prevent extreme heat from scorching and sterilizing the ground so that nothing will grow under or and around the place you have had your fire.

You'll need paper, dry grass, small twigs and limbs, or pieces of wood the size of your finger or smaller for kindling. Stack it loosely in your fire pit so that air can freely circulate under and though it. Then place slightly larger wood on top of that, and then larger, until you get to the size of about your wrist. Be careful not to pack it tightly. Light the kindling using a match or fire starter. You may need to fan it a little with your hat to get it going. Gradually add more wood. Do so before the fire gets too low.

Large logs aren't recommended by state, federal or county officials, as they don't always burn completely, are often difficult to extinguish, and the unburned logs that you leave behind can make the area look unsightly.

An easier way to start a fire is to squirt a little lighter fluid on your wood, following the directions on the container. You can also soak some twigs and kindling in the lighter fluid. Never use gasoline. This is dangerous and illegal. Never pour gasoline or lighter fluid on an already burning flame, coals, or hot ashes.

Once a fire is started, it's necessary to attend it closely until time to put it out. Never leave it unattended, even for a few minutes.

When a fire begins spreading, it can get out of control really quickly. Some of the larger brush fires have burned a thousand acres or more during the first two or three hours.

When leaving an area where you have set a fire, completely extinguish it before you leave. Douse it with enough water to put it out, then spread the ashes and douse it again. Be cautious, but touch the ashes, and when they're cool to the touch, the fire is completely out.

Many people try to extinguish flames with sand, but this doesn't always work because you may not get enough on the fire area to completely block all oxygen. It can smolder for hours and blaze up again.

In 2011, the Wallow Fire, which began in Arizona and spread into New Mexico, was the largest and most devastating fire in Arizona history. It started when two campers who thought their campfire was out, left the area. They stated that they thought it was safe because one of them threw a candy wrapper on the ashes to test it, and the wrapper didn't melt or burn.

When they tried to return several hours later, they couldn't get near their campsite because of the smoke and flames. One of two dogs that had been left tied up at the site was dead. Also, the campers didn't clear flammable debris from around the area where they started their campfire. Someone had previously built a fire there, and they had assumed that because of the existence of the fire ring, debris didn't need to be removed.

It may become necessary at some time for you to light a signal fire if you are injured or lost and awaiting rescue. The first step in starting a signal fire is to make sure that you're in a high enough place so that you can be seen from a wide area.

Clear the ground of brush and other combustibles around where you're going to light your fire for a distance of at least thirty to fifty feet if possible. This will minimize the danger of flying sparks spreading the blaze. As long as the area is cleared out, it isn't necessary to expend extra energy building a fire ring for your emergency signal fire.

Gather an ample amount of wood. You may need to keep your fire going for quite a while. It doesn't need to be a really large blaze, as even a moderate fire can be seen for many miles, especially at night. Also, you want to conserve your wood. You are going to expend a lot of energy gathering it, and there may not be too much of it nearby. You don't know how long your rescue will take, and you need to conserve your energy.

A daytime signal fire need not be large. However, flames are difficult to see during the day, so your fire should be smoky. All wood fires smoke, but you'll want yours to be extra smoky so that you'll attract attention. The best way to produce smoke is to use green wood. Once you get a dry wood fire going really well, add green branches and small green limbs. They'll make a large amount of smoke. You don't need to devastate an entire tree. Just break some of the smaller green branches and twigs from it. You don't need a lot. You can even pull up green brush. Live creosote (greasewood brush) is excellent for making smoke. Authorities are always watching for wild land fires, and your smoke will be picked up very soon. You'll need to keep adding dry wood to keep the fire going because the green wood won't burn by itself. Certain dry woods, such as palo verde, will smoke more than others.

It's against the law to cut green trees, and some green brush is also protected. However, if it comes to saving your life, it may be better to break this law and deal with the consequences later. Removing a few green limbs isn't a serious violation of the law, anyway. If you don't want to use brush or green limbs, you can always put water on the fire if you have enough water with you. Smoke made with water, however, is white and won't be as easily seen as black smoke. Also, this type of smoke won't last long. You'll also need to continue adding water, being careful not to add so much that your fire is extinguished.

Creosote Bush

It's not advisable to burn the tires or seats from your car unless there's absolutely no other way to save your life. At some point, you'll want to get your vehicle back to civilization and it's better that you don't have to have a set of wheels and tires hauled out to you. Also, you need to conserve your wood and energy. Tires won't ignite easily, and to make the fire hot enough to get them burning, you will need other combustibles to burn with them. This will take a lot of your wood, and you may not have much to begin with. Once burning, tires are very hard to extinguish. If you're rescued before they burn completely, you may not succeed in getting your fire out before you go. This further complicates your situation because you don't want to leave burning tires in the desert. By the time you are rescued, you may be too dehydrated, weak, and anxious to get out of there to want to deal with that situation. If you feel you absolutely must burn the tires, deflate them before you do so. There is at least one recorded case of a man who neglected to first deflate a tire before burning it, and it exploded. Sparks, rocks, hot coals, and debris were thrown into the air, seriously injuring him. Injured as well as stranded only compounds your problems.

Creosote leaves

Vehicle seats aren't always combustible, often are vinyl, and will melt rather than burn. Sometimes they can be composed partly of cotton and cloth, but usually there isn't enough to justify expending your energy to tear it apart. There is a lot of metal in seats, and it isn't generally worth the effort to remove them from the vehicle. Also, it's difficult to drive a car without a seat.

If you feel you must burn a seat, you can always cut any cloth and/or cotton and burnable materials from it, and take it to the fire. Don't forget to include any foam rubber. It provides a lot of smoke.

FLOODING

You shouldn't venture into the desert during the hot summer months, especially during the monsoon season of July and August. This is not only because of the extreme heat but because there is danger of flash flooding. Storms with torrential rains can blow up quickly. Even though the ground is very dry, the rains are so heavy that the water doesn't have time to sink into the ground, but it runs off into washes and low areas with great force. If you happen to be hiking or driving in its path, you can be washed away and even drowned. The water rushes down washes so quickly that it's usually not possible to outrun or out-drive it.

Not only are you in danger from the water, but there are often trees, cacti, sand, and other debris in the swift current that can dash against you and injure you, sometimes seriously.

The danger from these floods isn't just out in the wilds. Cities and towns are also in the desert, and many of the roads in urban areas pass through and across washes that flood from time to time. No matter where you're driving, if you see a flooded area, don't enter it. Don't drive across washes and low lying areas where you may be trapped by water. It takes only six to eight inches of rushing water to sweep your vehicle off a roadway. Flood water is muddy, and that makes it difficult to tell how deep it is or whether the pavement has been washed away underneath.

Every summer there are many motorists who disregard the danger from flash flood and end up having to be rescued. Frequently, their car is beyond repair or swept to a place where it's irretrievable. Often there is loss of life resulting from these incidents.

Photo by Jamie Colee

In Wickenburg, Arizona, during early July, 2012, a motorist was killed during a storm that produced two or three inches of rain in a matter of two or three hours, and consequently, flash flooding. The motorist entered a flooded wash with his SUV after being advised not to try to cross and in spite of signs that cautioned drivers not to enter. The vehicle was swept downstream, banging against trees and rocks, denting it, and sealing the doors, making it impossible to open them to escape. The SUV finally lodged in some trees, and when rescuers reached it, not only were the doors stuck closed, the windshield was broken. The driver was unresponsive. He was taken to a hospital by ambulance and was pronounced dead on arrival.

At the same time the above incident was occurring, another man only a few miles away drove into a flooded wash and had to be rescued by helicopter from the roof of his jeep. This individual was lucky. He escaped with his life.

During the same storm, our friend, Jamie Colee, captured on film still a third individual a few miles further away, who blundered headlong into a flooding wash near the town of Wittmann. This man drove around other cars that were parked waiting for the water to subside and slammed headlong into the flood. His vehicle became stranded out in the torrent. Maricopa County Sheriff's office was called, but they were unable to reach the location because of heavy traffic. A local man saw the danger of the motorist and brought his tractor. At the risk of his own life, he pulled the man and his car from the flooding wash. Although he was fortunate to escape without injury, the car was totally ruined, as are most vehicles caught in flood waters.

While these three incidents were taking place, rescuers in Phoenix and the surrounding area were busy helping other stranded motorists from flooded conditions.

This same scenario takes place every time there is a storm. Knowing what inevitably takes place, Fire and Rescue departments begin calling in extra people as soon as they know a brewing storm is going to be severe enough to cause flash flooding.

This is especially true in rural areas where there may not be enough manpower available to help every individual who is in trouble. It takes eight to twelve rescuers to accomplish a successful swift water rescue. Sometimes, the manpower may not be there and may have to be called in from another district, causing a delay in reaching victims. If you're in difficulty, you may find yourself on your own for quite a while until rescuers are able to reach you. By then, it may become a recovery rather than a rescue.

Most people who are rescued from floods in the southwest have gone around barricades and ignored warning signs. In some states, they're eligible to receive tickets, fines, and/or jail sentences and pay for their own rescue. In Arizona, all of this falls under what is called the "stupid motorist law."

During the monsoon season, caution should be exercised while driving through washes and low lying areas, even when it's not raining. Although there may be no precipitation where you are, washes and drainage systems are miles long, and floods may occur without you even seeing clouds. It may be storming a great distance from you. You may be down in a wash and have your view obstructed by hills and vegetation. Suddenly a wall of water appears, and you're trapped.

There are countless examples of drowning from flash floods, including those floods that occur when the storm is unseen and distant.

One of the worst disasters occurred in August, 1997, in Antelope Canyon, a narrow, deep, slot canyon in northern Arizona. Eleven people, the majority of whom were on a van camping tour, were drowned during a flash flood. It wasn't raining where the tourists were, and the clouds from the storm were impossible to see, not only because they were miles away, but because the canyon blocked a clear view of the sky.

The visitors suddenly heard a loud roar and saw the water bearing down upon them, but couldn't escape because the canyon walls were perpendicular and impossible to climb. The ladder they had descended on was washed away by the flood before they could reach it. The tour leader tried to pin several of them against the wall of the canyon and hold them there, but he was unable to do so because of the force of the water. He was also not able to hold onto any of them, and everyone, including the tour leader, was swept away. He managed to pull himself up onto a ledge, where he was found by rescuers in a semi-conscious condition. His ears, nose, eyes, and lungs were filled with sand, and the force of the water had ripped all clothing from his body. He was the sole survivor of all the visitors in the canyon when the flood hit.

There is danger all year of flash flooding in the southwestern deserts, but it doesn't happen often in the winter months, as the rains, for the most part, are gentle and have time to soak into the ground.

Flooding does occur during the winter when the rain continues for a period of days. This type of flooding gives warning, as you begin to notice water running and getting higher.

When camping on the desert, it's a good rule of thumb never to camp in a wash, no matter what the season. Washes exist because they've been carved by water. If there's any water, it will be running into the wash. As the preacher says, "plant your feet on higher ground."

During the flash flood season, it's common for housing and business areas in towns and cities to flood, as well as desert areas. The monsoons occur after a spell that has been hot and dry, and people tend to become excited when they see the rain and water and want to play in it.

Betty and a friend were on the way home from Phoenix when one of these monsoon gully washers hit. They were traveling on Grand Avenue, one of the main arteries leading to and from the Metropolitan area. The street began to fill with water and they pulled over by the gas pumps of a service station to wait out the storm. They sat there most of the night waiting and watching the local populace play in the water. About three in the morning, they were both amused and astounded to see two men in a rowboat float by.

In the summer of 2011, there were floods in areas of Phoenix that caused a lot of damage. Houses, vehicles, businesses, streets, and yards were underwater. The outlying town of

Anthem was hit especially hard. Walls of houses collapsed, and people had to be rescued. When firefighters and rescue units arrived on the scene, they found children and adults barefoot and playing in the floodwaters. There were so many of them that they hindered rescue efforts. Floodwater isn't clean. It has washed in from who knows where and is generally muddy and murky, making it impossible to see where you're stepping. The dirty water contains all sorts of bacteria and can even have substances such as animal or human feces from backed up sewers. Bacteria can get into an existing scratch or wound and infect you if you happen to cut yourself on debris such as cacti, glass, nails, boards, or sticks. Scorpions, insects, small snakes, and a host of other things may be swirling around in it. It can contain oil, gasoline, or other petroleum distillates. You may step into a hole from a washed out area and injure yourself.

Whenever there are people in any disaster area, there is danger that they may impede rescue efforts or get hurt and complicate matters by having to be rescued themselves. The best thing to do is to get out of the area if possible, and stay out of the way of emergency personnel.

SAND

Sand on the desert can be considered your worst enemy. Most of the desert is made up of sand. It's everywhere, and you or your vehicle can become trapped in it very easily.

Once trapped, it's extremely difficult to get out. Not only are you stranded out in the middle of nowhere and your outing possibly ruined, getting stuck can lead to a myriad of other types of distress. For example, trying to extricate your vehicle can use up your energy, exhausting you. If the weather is hot, the physical exertion can make it necessary to drink up all of your water, leaving you not only stranded, but dehydrated and in danger of all of the physical distress that dehydration can cause.

The extra strain of trying to get out of sand can cause your vehicle to throw a rod and can even ruin the engine. Tires can also be ruined due to spinning and overheating. There have been incidents where tires have caught on fire. We know of a group of people who, late on a rainy night, were coming from a desert party in a somewhat drunken state, when they became mired in a sandy wash. The driver of the vehicle gave it the gas, spinning the tires until they were smoking badly and about to erupt into a blaze, even though the sand was wet. Someone yelled, "I smell smoke! We're on fire!" Everyone bailed out except one individual who was too drunk to move. Fortunately, because the driver had jumped out too, was no longer spinning the wheels, and there was a lot of rain, the tires didn't actually burn. They were, however, completely ruined and the vehicle was hopelessly mired in the wet sand. It was a long, cold, process for the drenched group to figure out how they were going to get out of their predicament and get home.

If you become stranded in sand, you may be pretty much on your own, because many tow companies won't come to your aid if you're off highway. Often, insurances won't cover the expense, and most assuredly, it will be expensive. Even when help does arrive, sometimes vehicles can't be pulled out and are lost.

It's best to avoid driving into sand at all, but if you're going to, walk out onto it to gauge how loose and deep it is. The finer the sand and the deeper you sink into it walking, the more likely it is that you won't make it through with your vehicle. Even if you're following tracks or a road where others have gone, you can still get stuck.

After you've determined that it's safe to drive into the sand, don't stop for any reason. Keep going. If you stop, there's a good chance that you'll get stuck. If you have a four by four, shift into four wheel drive before entering the sand. If you wait until you're stuck before shifting, the chances of getting out are slim.

If, after all of your precautions, you find yourself getting mired down, the first thing to do is stop immediately when your tires begin spinning. The most common mistake people make is to try to drive out. This only spins the tires more and results in sinking further into the sand. It will take you clear up to the axles if you keep spinning. There is no exception to this. Once you feel yourself getting stuck, you can't drive out.

Once you're stuck, the first thing is to lighten the load. Passengers should get out, and any really heavy objects should be removed. Contrary to popular belief, making your vehicle heavier in sand won't give you traction, but will cause you to sink faster.

If you're not stuck too badly, it's possible that the passengers can push the vehicle enough to get through the sand. If the vehicle doesn't begin moving immediately, however, stop before you become too deeply entrenched.

Your next step is to jack up the drive wheels, front, rear, or both if you have a four wheel drive. Hopefully, you have brought something solid like a thick board on which to place the jack to prevent it from sinking in the sand. In the absence of a board, perhaps a flat rock can be used. Put rocks, brush, or anything else that might give you traction, under the wheels and in front of them. Make sure that a lot of the rocks are actually under the tires. Just having them in front of the tires isn't going to work. Now, try to drive out slowly. Don't spin your wheels or rev your engine. You may have to repeat this process several times before getting completely free.

If you can't free yourself from the sand, the best thing to do is to stay with your vehicle until help arrives, either from contacting someone to rescue you or your backup person missing you when you don't return or check in.

While a wash is running, or if the sand is still wet, quicksand can occur. Quicksand is sand that's super saturated with water and won't hold weight. The sand has to be wet or damp for quicksand to be present, but just because sand is wet, it doesn't mean that it's quicksand. It doesn't mean that it isn't, either. To make things even trickier, you can't always tell from looking that the sand is wet. Sometimes it will be dry, but there will be a wet patch in the dry sand. This is a sign of possible quicksand, as quicksand dries up last. Jim learned this when he was crossing a river on foot and stepped from dry into wet sand and sank up to his waist.

Contrary to what you see in the movies, quicksand in desert areas tends to be quick. You don't usually sink slowly, waving your arms and screaming for help. Generally, you sink rapidly. However, on the upside, bedrock is usually just a few feet down, so you don't often sink in over your head like in the movies, although it can happen. At times, though, bedrock can be six or more feet deep. Children are in greater danger than adults because they're smaller.

Our advice is to stay out of washes that look damp, wet, or have been or are running, even a little bit. Quicksand isn't that rare an occurrence and shouldn't be taken lightly. If you do venture through wet or damp sand and don't get caught in quicksand, remember that it can move. If you come back later and expect to cross the same wet sand, you may find that it has turned to quicksand.

If you get stuck in quicksand, you can usually get out by yourself. Above all, don't panic. Just walk out. It's not easy because the mud, sand and water are thick, and walking is difficult. If you're sinking slowly, lie down. You'll sink more slowly that way because you have more surface area than just your feet. At times, but not always, you may be able to sort of swim out. It depends on how thick or thin the quicksand is or if it has a suction to it. You may be able to lie down in the sand and swim if you are lucky. If you are very deep and someone else is trying to help you out, they shouldn't come close to you and should be careful not to fall in, too. The rescuer should extend a rope, towel, long stick, trousers or other clothing (even tied together, shoelaces probably won't work) to the victim and help him escape that way.

If your vehicle becomes mired in quicksand, it can be a very different story. Usually it gets ruined. If you're lucky, bedrock may be near the surface. If it isn't, your vehicle may be lost. If you're traveling with other vehicles, you may be able to attach a tow rope to yours and be towed out. If you're alone, there's little you can do.

Our dad once got stuck in quicksand in his Willys Jeep in the Santa Maria River, west of Bagdad, Arizona. The jeep had a fairly solid bottom and it floated long enough for others in his party to attach tow straps to it and pull it out. There are pictures of him standing in the back of the jeep with his hands on his hips watching people attach the tow line.

When we said sand on the desert is everywhere, we mean that literally. At times, it's not only on the ground but in the atmosphere. During the monsoon season, the southwest is prone to huge storms that blow sand and dust and often cause a lot of damage to landscapes, buildings, vehicles and other property. These storms can blow trees, large cacti, and power lines down. Often the sand and dust are so thick that visibility is reduced to zero.

These dust storms are usually associated with rain, but can occur without it. They generally happen during late afternoons, but sometimes occur at night or in the morning. If they hit during daylight hours, you'll be able to see a wall of dust approaching in the distance. If it looks brown or dust colored, it's usually not far away and you have only about thirty minutes, at most, to prepare. If it appears very dark, or almost black, it will probably take longer to reach you, or may not even hit at all where you are.

Dust storms can be especially dangerous when you're driving because your visibility is greatly reduced. If you see one coming, the best thing to do is get completely off the road a safe distance, if you can, and wait the storm out in your vehicle. It will usually last only about thirty to forty five minutes, at most.

If you're unexpectedly caught in the storm and are driving, you need to pull over to the shoulder of the road, and get as far off the roadway as possible. Turn off your lights if you have them on. Many times, there have been multiple car pileups because other drivers have seen lights and assumed the car ahead of them was on the roadway and moving. They hit them from behind and were hit in turn by other vehicles. Sometimes drivers have not pulled over, but just stopped in the middle of the road or slowed down to a crawl and were hit. Some of these pileups have involved up to fifty vehicles. One involved over a hundred.

If you're not driving, you should seek cover. Get inside a building or vehicle if either is nearby. If you're out on the desert and can't get to shelter, try to get behind a dirt bank, the lee side of a hill, a large boulder, or some other solid object. Try to stay out from under trees and away from saguaro cacti. Trees and saguaros are frequently uprooted, and branches and limbs from both of these can be blown off and land on you. If nothing else, lay flat on the ground. This latter is a last resort, as the ground may be hot and burn you, but it's better than being hit full force by flying debris and sand.

Try not to breathe in the dust if you're caught outside during one of these storms. The fungi that cause valley fever are commonly found in the dirt and can be breathed in whenever the soil is disturbed or blown around. During the past few years, dust storms have become more severe because of drought, and incidences of valley fever have risen accordingly. If you have a bandana, scarf, or other cloth that you can put to your nose and mouth to breathe through, it will help cut your chances of contracting this illness. If possible, you should dampen the cloth.

Severe sandstorms have been known to ruin windshields and paint jobs on vehicles. Betty and her husband had to replace the windshield and grill of a brand new car after one such misadventure near Indio, California. Think what it can do to your skin! If possible, cover any exposed part of your body, and protect your eyes if you're caught out during a sandstorm.

HIKING AND BACKPACKING

Although we've covered some of the basic needs of hikers throughout this book, there is still a little more to be said.

If you're going to be carrying a pack, it's essential that you select the proper kind for the hike you'll be making. We don't mean color. We mean utilitarian. We know a seasoned back country wilderness guide who went with some inexperienced hikers to help them pick out packs. Their main concern was that their new packs would be color coordinated with their outfits.

There are many types of packs (in many different colors) to choose from. In selecting one, it's best to take an experienced hiker with you, or go to an outdoor store and work with the staff to find one that will fit your particular needs and body size. For example, if you're only going to be gone for a few hours or part of the day, you don't need a gigantic pack with a frame reaching above your head. A simple rucksack or small pack will do for that type of outing. Most experienced hikers own several types of packs so they'll have an appropriate one for their outing.

According to most backpackers and back country guides that we have spoken with, the biggest challenge for hikers is to carry all their essentials without having too heavy a load to be carried for the distance that they may be going.

Although every hike is different and the required gear may differ from trip to trip, there are certain things that you need to take whenever you go out. These include, but are not limited to, adequate water and food, a first aid kit, cell phone, compass, GPS if you have one, sunscreen, matches, and a pocket knife.

The longer your trip, the more supplies you'll need and the more attention will have to be given to weight and what may be absolutely necessary or not necessary. Although a pack loaded with gear and supplies may not seem heavy at first, it can become more and more of a load as you progress through the day, or days. You'll get tired, and what had seemed all right at first can become much too heavy. It's better to decide what to discard before you get out on the trail. We've seen some of our back country wilderness guide friends choose between two almost identical items based on one being a few ounces lighter than another.

Being in good physical condition is essential for any type of serious hike. You'll need to know your limitations and capabilities very well. Before attempting to take a long trek, you should condition yourself by making smaller hikes. You'll need to do strengthening and endurance exercises such as weight lifting, swimming and jogging.

Diet is important in any physical fitness program, but it's especially so if you're going to be trekking for an extended period of time. Not only should you have a good diet while training, but if you're taking an extended hike, you should train with basically the same types of foods you'll be eating on your trip. A sudden major change in diet, especially when you're exerting yourself, will often result in becoming ill. This isn't what you want to have happen on the trail.

Extra caution needs to be taken when hiking in steep, mountainous areas. In these places, there are all sorts of feats that you may want to attempt and all sorts of situations you can find yourself in if you try some of these things without proper training, preparation, and equipment. A surprising number of people have had to be rescued because they attempted to scale and descend from cliffs and mountains that required rappelling equipment that hikers didn't have with them. They also have gotten trapped on mountainsides and ledges. Many have been injured, often seriously. Far too many of these incidents have resulted in fatalities, both of hikers and rescuers.

In July, 2013, a rescuer was killed trying to get a man off Mt. Charleston, near Las Vegas, Nevada. The hiker had ignored signs declaring the area off limits. He became stranded and disoriented. The rescuer was lowered to him from a helicopter, attached a safety harness to both of them, and gave the order to pull them up. During this process, the harness became detached from the officer, and he fell to his death.

One rescuer near Phoenix was killed by a helicopter rotor blade while attempting a mountainside rescue.

Most areas accessible to hikers have trails. It's essential to stay on them, and obey all off-limits and warning signs. The majority of mountain rescues occur because hikers have left the trails and attempted to do things beyond their knowledge and capabilities.

WATER SAFETY

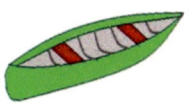
While water safety isn't within the major scope of this book, there are a few things that you should know about some of the lakes and reservoirs on the southwestern deserts. Complete safety information and laws and regulations for individual areas can be viewed online or from various publications and pamphlets issued by the Game and Fish Department and the Department of Parks and Recreation.

The southwest has many lakes and reservoirs that are used by people who come to enjoy the desert. While most people from other areas know a lot about safety in water, the desert lakes and reservoirs can be somewhat different from other areas, and the rules can be slightly different, as well.

Almost all lakes in the southwest are man-made. They're flooded desert land and have been formed by the building of dams and water being channeled from some other area into basins that will hold water and form lakes. Often, the major volume of water has been channeled from a distant source, as in the case of Lake Pleasant. Most of the water in that lake has been brought by canal from the Colorado River, a distance of about two hundred miles.

The bottoms of these man-made lakes can be very different from the bottoms of natural lakes because of the rough and uneven terrain that the water has covered. In most natural lakes, the bottom slopes downward from the beach, becoming gradually deeper. Because desert lakes have mostly been formed from damming up an area and flooding it, the bottom doesn't always have the gradual slope from shallow to deep. Water covers hills, washes, cliffs, cacti, brush, trees, and even houses. You can be wading along the shoreline in ankle deep water and suddenly find that you have stepped off a cliff and are in over your head.

Water can be three feet deep in one place and over a hundred feet deep just a few yards away.

A volunteer worker at Lake Pleasant tells of warning a group of people wading along the shore with their children about this, and advised using life jackets if the people weren't swimmers. His warnings were ignored, and about an hour later he saw rescue crews pulling the drowned body of a young boy from the water.

When desert lakes were being formed, vegetation from what was to become the bottom of the lake was mostly not cleared. There are remnants of cacti, brush, trees, large rocks, boulders and sometimes buildings on the bottom. Some of the lakes are partially drained during certain seasons and the water diverted for use in areas of major population. When the lakes are refilled, sometimes the shoreline will be higher than it was previously and will be covering even more cacti and brush as well as vegetation that has grown while the water was low.

While a lot of vegetation has biodegraded in older parts of lakes, not all of it has, and you can't always see it. It's easy to step on this and fresh brush and cacti that have been newly covered by the water, as well as sharp rocks, fish hooks, and other trash and debris. We recommend that you wear tennis or water shoes when wading, and if you are in deeper water, watch out for trees that may be just under the surface.

Because of the lack of sandy beaches, vehicles can often be driven right up to the water's edge. What used to be desert hills often have turned into steep banks around the shore of lakes when they were flooded. Always set your emergency brake, and block the tires with a rock if you are parking on one of these slopes. More than one vehicle has jumped out of gear or somehow or other rolled into the lake. Often, these vehicles are completely covered with water and unsalvageable.

A family of four hiked several miles to our stable, desperate for help because they had parked on a hill, their car had rolled into the lake and was completely submerged. They called for help and got the vehicle out, but it was ruined.

Several weeks later, a tour of European young people rode horseback with us to the lake for a swim, but instead spent their swimming time watching a tow truck pull a totally submerged pickup truck from the water.

Because of hidden boulders, the changing depth of the water and other obstructions, diving off banks and cliffs is dangerous. Even if you know how deep the water is on one occasion, it can be a very different depth just a few days or weeks later, because, as mentioned previously, water is constantly being drained and diverted for use in other areas. At times, water levels become higher when more water is being brought into the lake.

Occasionally, rattlesnakes are encountered along the shoreline because water tends to attract them. Furthermore, they swim. Our dad told of one trying to get into his boat while he and a friend were on Lake Pleasant. The snake was up over the side of the boat and had to be killed with an oar. This was no easy feat, as it was squiggling, and the occupants of the boat were flailing wildly with the oars trying to hit their target.

Unless there is immediate danger of being bitten by a snake, the best thing to do is get away from it and notify an authority, such as a Park Ranger. It may be helpful to leave one of your party to watch from a safe distance where the snake is headed, because it probably won't be right there when help arrives. The snake can then be removed and won't be a danger to others who may stumble across it.

Because of the heat and mild winters in the southwestern United States, swimming pools are very popular as a way to cool off and also because you can swim most of the year. The large number of pools increase the chances of drowning and has resulted in a large number of fatalities in children under the age of fifteen. Whenever you're near a pool or any source of water, it's essential to carefully watch your children. The majority of small children who drown in swimming pools have only been out of sight of adults for a few minutes. Children love swimming pools and seem to head directly to any nearby water when they get away from their parents and guardians. It only takes a few minutes for them to drown. Even when children survive a near drowning incident, they may sustain serious brain damage. There are many young people who are now impaired so badly that they'll never function normally again after almost drowning.

The only way to prevent these accidents from happening is to be prepared for them in advance. Children can be taught to swim at a very early age, and that, aside from constant surveillance, is your best defense.

Fence your pool, and keep the gates closed and locked. Children can climb fences and squeeze through openings that would astonish any adult, so make the fence completely impenetrable to them. This is a tall order. There have been instances where children have drowned, and it was never understood how they got into the pool area. Children have been put down for naps and have slipped out of their beds, through doors that were thought to be locked and into the water. Every imaginable scenario has taken place. You simply can't be too careful.

PETS AND ANIMALS

Most pets become part of the family and it's natural to want to include them in the family fun and outings. Some pets will enjoy an outing. Others won't.

Birds, for example, are generally better off left at home with someone to watch them while you're gone. If you take them with you, they'll probably take more care than when you're at home. They're usually in cages that are bulky to move or transport. Their drinking water spills easily on bumpy roads, birdseed can spill out of containers, making a mess in your vehicle, and the birds are generally uncomfortable. If you're going in your motor home or camper, it may be more feasible to take them.

Birds seem to easily escape from their cages when they're on camping trips. We've seen canaries, parakeets, and other types of birds that have apparently escaped from their owners flying around the desert. It's impossible to catch or rescue them. They're not equipped to survive on their own in the wild.

Cats are also not good to bring along on a camping trip. If you bring them, you'll probably have to confine them to a cage or kennel. As almost every cat owner knows, they don't always do well on a leash and all too frequently go ballistic in a vehicle. If they're turned loose, they tend to not return to a campsite.

Cats are very adaptable, independent, are natural hunters, and can often survive on their own. The desert is full of feral cats that were once somebody's loved pet. Across from our stable is a mountain with a large number of feral cats living on it that we call Cat Mountain. On the other side of our establishment is a wash full of them that we call Cat Canyon.

One case of a domestic cat gone feral comes immediately to our minds. It happened several years ago when a family came to us in their motor home to camp for a week. They brought their cat, who had been living with them for about eight years. This cat was declawed, fat, lazy, lovable, and normally never left his living room in Denver. He didn't leave the motor home, either, until the last day when the family was getting ready to go home. The cat suddenly jumped up, bolted out the door and refused to come back, despite calls from his family and fresh food being set out for him. He seemed to be having a ball and eventually ran into the desert. His heartbroken family finally had to leave without him.

The cat never came back into the stable area and somehow managed to survive on the desert for at least a year. He was often seen when we were riding out onto the trail, but would never come to us. Then, we didn't see him anymore. Hopefully, he is still alive out there.

The pet that most frequently accompanies their owners into the desert is the dog. Your dog, of all pets, is the one most likely to enjoy an outing, but there are precautions that should be taken.

Before letting your dog run free on the desert, you need to check for leash laws in the area where you'll camping when he's with you.

One of the most common mishaps on outings with dogs is that they can become lost. Over the years, we've had many people stop by our stable searching for their dogs. Often they put up signs throughout the area offering monetary rewards for their return. Sometimes they're located, frequently they aren't. In any case, the owners are heartbroken and probably the dog is, too.

Unlike cats, dogs that aren't actually raised in the desert often don't survive there. Sometimes they manage to make their way to someone's camp, a ranch house, or other place of human habitation, and if they're lucky, the people there will take care of them and try to locate their family. All too often, however, these dogs are ignored and left to starve to death or fall prey to other animals such as coyotes or javalinas. Sometimes people will shoot them.

One of the worst things that can happen to lost dogs is that they will survive and join wild dogs who roam the desert in packs.

These animals, owing to the fact that they have to survive, usually become outlaws and will raid campgrounds, hunt and kill wildlife. and even rancher's calves. They'll sneak into people's yards and kill chickens and other domestic animals that they can eat. They can be dangerous to humans because they often become vicious, and because they were once domestic, they aren't afraid of people.

When these dog packs become too aggressive, local folks will often hunt and shoot them or will call animal control to try to round them up. They almost never make good pets again after their experiences in the wild.

The best thing to do is to keep your dog nearby and within hearing distance so you can keep track of him. If he gets excited and takes off, such as when he sniffs a rabbit and gives chase, this may be difficult to do. For this reason, he should be wearing identification on his collar or have a chip. These can be helpful, but aren't guarantees of having a dog returned to you, as collars can slip off in brush, or if rescued, the rescuers may not search for a chip. Also, many people, upon finding a dog in the desert will pick him up and take him home to live with them without even bothering to search for his family. Or they may find a dog that isn't even lost and take him to a shelter.

For example, a miner who lived in the desert near us always took his dog, Charlie, with him as he went about his daily search for gold.

Charlie spent his nights inside the camper with his owner and by morning would need exercise, so the prospector would let him out at the top of a hill above the area where he was mining. Charlie would race to the bottom of the hill and eagerly meet his owner's truck there.

One morning, the miner got to his claim at the bottom of the hill and Charlie wasn't there. A week later, the dog was located at a shelter in Phoenix. It was fifty miles from where he disappeared. Someone, apparently thinking he was lost, had dropped him off there. Charlie had been wearing a collar with his identification and also had a chip that no one thought to look for. The collar was missing. The prospector and Charlie were both very lucky to find each other again. Many stories like this don't have a happy ending.

We saw another story with a happy ending on the evening news. A dog and his owner were enjoying an outing on the desert, and the dog was happily chasing rabbits. They became separated and the owner searched and called in vain for his pet.

Weeks later, the dog was found in Pennsylvania. Someone had thought to look for his identification chip. No one knows how he got from Arizona to Pennsylvania.

Not only do you have to guard your dog from getting lost, but you need to protect him from the environment when you're on your outing. Dogs that aren't raised in the country may have a difficult time once they're out in the wild. They don't always understand about the terrain or cacti and frequently become covered in cactus thorns or become footsore from the rocks. You can use the pliers in your tool kit to pull out any thorns or stickers.

Rattlesnakes are a danger to dogs. Your dog should receive rattlesnake vaccine once a year, whether he's going into the desert or is never going to leave his back yard. Rattlesnakes can be anywhere. Even in the city, the fire department removes quite a few snakes from back yards. Dogs love to run up to them and sniff, bark, or play. Snakes seem to love to bite them. With the vaccine, there is little or no danger to the dog if it's bitten. The vaccine will protect dogs from the bites of every type of rattlesnake except the Mojave, which has two types of venom.

Courses in rattlesnake training are widely offered throughout the southwest, and we recommend that your dog have these classes. In these courses, canines are conditioned to fear snakes and run away rather than approach, bark, attack, try to play with them, or exhibit various other reactions dogs may have to rattlesnakes. Check with your local fish and game office to find times and locations in your area that hold rattlesnake training classes.

Whatever animal you may take with you into the desert, remember that he, just like you, will need extra water and may have special food requirements or medications, and you'll need to plan accordingly.

FIREARMS

Target shooting is a popular activity on the desert. This can be a lot of fun if done in the right way and in the proper place, but if done improperly it can lead to a lot of misery and heartache. It isn't within the scope of this book to conduct a gun safety course, but because of the danger and number of firearms being taken to the desert, gun safety does need to be addressed.

We recommend an NRA or other safety course before taking a gun out to shoot. A great number of accidents could be prevented if owners of firearms were informed and knew how to use them. Also, common sense and responsibility are often thrown to the winds when people bring their guns on their outings, especially if they're combining guns with alcohol or other substances.

Irresponsible shooters have left shotgun and other caliber shells littering the desert, cacti riddled with bullet holes and dying, and dead wild life from birds to burros. There are areas where almost every road sign has at least two or three bullet holes and usually more. We've seen stock tanks shot to pieces with no water in them for the animals to drink, vehicles parked by the side of the road with bullet holes in them, windmills destroyed, ranchers' cattle, horses, and even people, accidentally shot.

Stray bullets have cut through the tops of mesquite trees right at our stable and one even came through the kitchen wall missing Betty's grandson's head by inches. This happened at night. The shooter apparently didn't realize or care that it's illegal to shoot at night, and foolish and illegal to shoot at or near buildings or human habitations.

A lot of cacti and wild life are considered endangered, and all are legally protected. There are fines for shooting animals without a license and for destroying plant life. There are hefty penalties for leaving your shell casings on the ground, shooting ranch animals, and destroying ranch equipment. And if you accidentally shoot a person, your own life can be destroyed as well as that of your victim.

We recommend that you target shoot at one of the excellent shooting facilities located throughout the southwest, such as the Ben Avery gun range north of Phoenix.

If you do shoot out on the desert, you should first check with the land agency responsible for the area where you'll be shooting to see that there isn't a fire ban and that shooting is allowed. Shooting isn't permitted during fire bans, which are usually in force during the hot, dry summer months.

Next, select an isolated area. Bullets from most guns carry further than people may realize. A bullet from a high powered rifle, such as a .30.30, .270, .308, .30.06, and similar caliber fire arms can carry up to three to five miles. Even a .22 rifle shooting .22 long rifle bullets can carry up to a mile. Assault rifles can carry up to two miles. Trees and brush can hide animals and people from view, and many times both humans and livestock have been accidentally shot.

It's best to use a target purchased at a gun shop or something similar that you have made yourself.

When setting up your target, make sure there are no weeds or brush around the target area. Sparks from steel jacketed bullets have been known to cause fires. In 2010, in Utah, 2,300 people had to be evacuated from their homes because of such a fire. By early June, 2013, there had been eight known fires caused by firearms that year in Arizona.

Since cacti and other vegetation, as well as wildlife, cattle, and other livestock are protected by law, it's never a wise choice to use them as targets. Too often, tin and aluminum cans and other objects have been used for targets and left to litter the desert. If you use cans and other objects, pick them up and take them with you when you leave. Glass bottles, crockery, plates and similar items should never be used as targets. There are vast areas of desert that have been ruined this way. Even if you try to clean up your mess when you go, it's impossible to pick up all of the shards. Furthermore, glass biodegrades so slowly that it will be there for generations.

Large appliances such as old refrigerators, washers, dryers, stoves, and so forth are often carted off to the desert, riddled with bullets and left there. We had our washing machine set up outside at our stable and people came right into our yard and shot it full of holes. Shooting a washer that a group of cowboys are depending on to do their laundry may not be a good idea.

Also, it happens all too frequently that if a vehicle breaks down and is left by the side of the road while the owner goes for help, it gets used for target practice.

In setting up a proper target, you'll need a backdrop such as a hill, a dirt bank, or the edge of a wash or cliff to stop the bullets. You don't know who is around but out of sight that your bullets may hit. Your backdrop should have no large boulders or anything that bullets can ricochet from. Stand a good distance back from your target, as bullets have been known to ricochet even off small rocks and hit the shooter or an innocent bystander.

Keep all children and others well behind the shooter. Very small children shouldn't be taken on target shooting trips. A death occurred in Arizona when a four year old girl was unattended and suddenly darted out in front of her mother's gun just as her mother pulled the trigger.

Exploding targets and incendiary bullets should never be used. In 2012, one of Arizona's largest wildfires, the Sunflower fire, was started by a group of young men on a bachelor party when one of them loaded an incendiary bullet into his shotgun. By the time the blaze was completely contained, about 18,000 acres had been burned.

Shell casings can be found littering vast areas of the desert. Most of these are the plastic casings from shotguns, which don't biodegrade easily and deface the earth for years. Always pick up all shell casings after your shooting session.

Most gun accidents on the desert involve alcohol or other drugs. Alcohol, drugs, and guns definitely don't mix, no matter how much fun you're having or how badly you need to relax and get away from it all for the day or weekend.

MINING AREAS

Anyone recreating on the desert will sooner or later find themselves in the vicinity of old mines and shafts. These can be highly dangerous.

The Bureau of Land Management, most state governments, and volunteer agencies have made a concentrated effort to fence or seal off old mines and to fill in old shafts located on Federal and state lands, but there are still many they haven't yet been able to deal with. It has been estimated that in the combined states of California, Arizona, Nevada, Utah, and New Mexico there are in excess of a half million abandoned mine sites. Of these, only about a quarter of a million have been identified and located.

During the 1970's, incidents of deaths and injuries in and around these old mines began making the news. There were only a few at first, but as the population of the southwest increased, the number of victims grew. Mining officials and state and Federal agencies began to become alarmed at the certainty of growing numbers of accidents as the population continued to burgeon, and as a result, legislation at both the state and Federal levels was passed, and funding was appropriated for identifying and closing off these areas. Laws were established for those who were closing mines to make sure they were safe and inaccessible to the public. Programs to educate people about the danger of these mines were put in place.

Due to the increasing number of deaths and accidents at the sites of both active and abandoned mines, the Arizona State Mine Inspector's Office (ASMI) and the National Mine Safety and Health Administration (MSHA) have designated the week of April 27-May 1, as Mine Safety Awareness Week. The week is designed to educate and raise awareness that mines are not made for recreating and are unsafe to play in. The theme for the week is "Stay Out, Stay Alive!"

The ASMI also created the Abandoned Mines Educational Program to introduce students to mine safety and help them to understand what accidents can happen on mining property and what the dangers are. By the time the course is finished, the students should know the following:

Never play in or explore abandoned mines.
Never play around active mines
Never jump into quarry pits or ponds in or around mines
Never swim in rock quarries or gravel/sand pits
Never climb on rock or gravel piles in mining areas
Notify authorities if a mine site is found unmarked.

Old mine tunnels are especially dangerous. Supporting beams and timbers can be rotten, and the walls and ceilings tend to crumble and cave in easily. They can be so fragile that just the jarring of your feet as you walk through them can cause them to cave in. Sometimes there are shafts in the tunnels that go hundreds of feet straight down. You may not see these in the dark and fall in.

Often, there are poisonous gasses present in these tunnels. They are odorless. There is no way to detect them, and you won't know they're there until you are overcome by them. By then, it's too late to escape. Early miners carried canaries in cages to detect these gasses. Birds are more sensitive to them than people. If the canary suddenly dropped dead, the miners fled immediately if they were still able to do so. Miners also used candles in their hard hats both for light and to measure oxygen levels. If there was suddenly a large concentration of carbon dioxide, their candle would go out, indicating an absence of oxygen. They could possibly make it to safety. However, modern recreators usually don't run around the desert with canaries in cages or candles, so the best precaution you can take is to stay out of mine tunnels.

Mine tunnels don't have to be old or abandoned to collect poisonous gasses. In 2009, two miners in Prescott, Arizona, died in the tunnel they dug when poisonous gasses collected there.

Besides poisonous gasses, there can be annoying, and even dangerous, critters lurking in old mines. Pack rats love to live in these places, and their nests are full of sticks, cacti, and other debris. The cacti usually get scattered over a wide area and it's very easy to brush against it, step on it, stir it up in the dust, and get stuck with it. Some cacti used in these nests have very fine, minute thorns, and just by walking through the tunnel, you can breathe them in. It's really irritating when you find that they're in your nose or in your collar. It feels a lot like you're working with fiberglass insulation, only worse. Pack rats will carry in old pieces of glass, tin cans, and other items that can hurt you. Once, we found wads and wads of old cotton in one of these nests. It looked like the rats had found an old mattress and carried most of it with them to help make their house.

By now, it's obvious where we're going with this, and so it should be unnecessary to mention bats that carry rabies, spiders, scorpions, centipedes, various types of snakes and other critters that could possibly make their homes in old tunnels. It's even been reported that bobcats and mountain lions have used old mines as their dens.

The danger from rattlesnakes in these old mines is high. They are attracted to them partly because of the other small animals living there that can provide a food source. In summer, they crawl into them to escape the heat, and in winter they hibernate in them. A mining group was attempting to reopen a network of old mine tunnels near Congress, Arizona. It was in the early spring, and it was chilly. Unknown to them, the tunnels were filled with hibernating snakes that no one saw while exploring in the dark with only flashlights for illumination. A few days later, when the weather warmed up, the men were horrified to see huge rattlesnakes crawling from the mine they had been probing around in. They killed well over a dozen of these reptiles. A lot of them got away.

It's not just the tunnels that are dangerous. There are mine shafts all over the desert, some several hundred feet deep. Often, these are surrounded by brush and vegetation and are not easily seen or can crumble if you're too close to the edge. People, animals, and even vehicles fall into them. These accidents can be serious or fatal.

Once, when Betty and her husband were out on horseback gathering cattle with a rancher, one of the cattle dogs suddenly dropped from sight. It was as though the ground had swallowed him. Upon riding their horses over to where the animal had disappeared, it was discovered that there was an old mine shaft surrounded by brush and cacti, and the dog had fallen into it. Fortunately, he was rescued unharmed when one of the cowboys lowered himself into the twenty foot deep shaft with a lariat rope and lifted him out. Even though they had ridden through the area for many years, the brush was so thick and the shaft so well hidden, that none of the cowboys had ever seen it before.

Some are not as fortunate as the dog. Near Dolan Springs, Arizona, two sisters, ages ten and thirteen years old, were following their father on an ATV. When he arrived at their destination and the girls didn't show up, the dad notified authorities. The quad was tracked to an abandoned mine shaft that had been invisible due to the growth of surrounding brush. At the bottom of the one hundred twenty-five foot deep shaft, lay the two girls and the quad. The ten year old was rescued and transported in critical condition to University Medical Center in Las Vegas, Nevada, but the thirteen year old was pronounced dead at the scene.

Sometimes, victims and bodies can't be pulled from these old shafts. One especially grisly case in point is that of a twenty-eight year old man who fell into a 190 foot deep shaft in Jersey Valley, Nevada, in March, 2011. He had been working nearby with a geothermal drilling crew and during his off hours was visiting the mining area with two friends. They were looking down into an old shaft, when the edge gave way and he fell. Rescuers were unable to reach him because the sides of the shaft were crumbling, and large rocks were falling on their heads, endangering their lives. The rescue was called off, even though the man was still alive and suffering from major head injuries. He was monitored until his heart stopped beating, and he was pronounced dead.

Although most dynamite and explosives in old mines have been biodegraded or removed, occasionally some old dynamite that was overlooked can still be found. It can be very dangerous because the nitroglycerine can have leaked out, forming crystals on the outside of the dynamite. Nitroglycerine is very unstable, explosive, and volatile. If one of the crystals is broken, jarred, or has a heat source close to it, it will explode. If you happen to jar it or break a crystal while walking past it, or if you step on it inadvertently, there will definitely be an explosion.

Never touch or pick up old dynamite that you find. Report it immediately to the authorities so that people or wild animals won't be injured or killed if they should happen upon it.

It may be surprising to learn that all old, abandoned mines are not in remote areas. During the past several decades, cities and towns in the southwest have grown not only in population but in area. Places that were out in the countryside are now near the city limits or even inside them. Old mine sites have sometimes been overlooked and not sealed off or filled in. They are still a danger to the public.

For example, a man riding a quad in an undeveloped area within the city limits of Peoria, Arizona, unknowingly got too close to an old shaft and the quad fell into it and tipped over, trapping him underneath in the bottom of the shaft. Luckily, he was rescued with non-life-threatening injuries. This is by no means an isolated incident. People have had similar experiences within the city limits of Phoenix and other towns.

The best way to prevent mishaps with abandoned mine shafts is to be very careful when hiking. Don't step where you can't see, and stay away from brushy, overgrown areas. If you do see an old shaft, don't approach it or get very close to the edge in case it's unstable or crumbly. When riding recreational vehicles, adhere to laws by staying on existing, designated trails. The laws have been put in place not only to protect the environment, but to protect you. You should report any unmarked or unfenced mine shafts to authorities, as perhaps they've been overlooked and not yet documented.

Section III

DESERT ANIMALS

By Jim Koning

There are so many animals, critters, and insects living on the desert that we can only cover the most common, most venomous, and potentially dangerous ones. Some of these critters are encountered only rarely, while some are seen more often. There is a rule to follow when encountering these animals: *if at all possible, leave them alone to go about their own business.* This applies to all animals whether they be snakes, small animals like squirrels, skunks, or larger animals like coyotes, foxes, bobcats, and the like. Always remember that these wild critters may be seen at any time while out camping, hiking, and having fun on the desert. They may also be encountered if you're living in an outlying area, and even in town.

It's important to understand these wild animals in order to help you avoid an unpleasant encounter with them. Some of these critters can ruin more than just your day if you anger or scare one. Most, if not all the wild animals and crawling critters that roam the desert areas of North America are not aggressive (with the exception of Africanized bees). They won't go out of their way to attack a human under normal circumstances. Of course, they are wild things and there are exceptions, like if you come close to a mother animal with young, if you come upon them suddenly and surprise them, or if they have an illness like rabies, which affects their brain. *Under no circumstance should you approach any animal in the wild. They might feel threatened and become aggressive, and some of them may be diseased. Some animals are venomous.*

Very rarely, you may see a wild animal that is aggressive by nature. You don't want to come close to one of these. They are living beings and like all living things have individual personalities and emotions. They should be left alone. Observe them from a safe distance.

Sometimes people who live in outlying areas or camp on the desert like to set out food for the wildlife. While it's nice to watch the wild animals, feeding them isn't a good idea for several reasons. For example, setting out food and water will attract unwanted animals such as rattlesnakes. They'll come not only for the water but for the rodents and other small animals they feed on.

Rodents such as field mice and packrats that come for food and water carry all sorts of diseases that may be passed on to pets and humans. These small creatures find their way into your campsite or house, are a real nuisance, and are hard to get rid of. Any water left out will also attract scorpions and insects that venomous spiders such as black widows feed on. You don't want these in your camp or house. The food and water will also bring animals like javelinas, bobcats, coyotes, and other larger animals that are potentially dangerous to your pets, other people's pets, yourself, and your neighbors.

These animals can also come to depend on the food that you're putting out. While they may not lose their ability to hunt, like any other living thing, they'll follow the path of least resistance, and go where the food is easiest to get. If for any reason they stop being fed, they'll become a nuisance trying to find the food they're used to getting. They'll have lost much of their fear of humans, and some of the larger animals may become aggressive if you're outside without food for them.

One other danger is encountering an animal with rabies. This is fairly rare, but happens more often than one would think. According to the Center for Disease Control, 40,000 people in the United States are exposed each year and receive rabies vaccine. Many of these are in the southwest. The Arizona Department of Health Services states that an average of 30 people per year are exposed to rabies in Arizona. The New Mexico CDC said that in 2012, they were involved in 80 cases of PEP (post exposure prophylactic) shots, but the number of people who receive them was higher because many were being treated by private physicians.

The principle hosts of rabies in the desert are bats, skunks, and foxes. Bats are considered the number one carrier of rabies in desert areas, although relatively few bats have it. All mammals can get rabies, and all mammals die from it. If an animal other than a bat, skunk, or fox has it, it has contracted it from one of these animals.

Rabies is a deadly virus spread to people from the saliva of an infected animal, usually, but not always, through a bite. The virus travels along the nerves reaching the central nervous system and then travels to the brain causing brain swelling (encephalitis) and ultimately death. Rabies can show up from ten days to several months after exposure from a bite.

After a rabid animal bites, rabies shots or post exposure prophylactic (PEP) treatments are given to prevent rabies from developing. These shots should be given as soon as possible after exposure, but health authorities such as the Center for Disease Control, recommend getting them regardless of the time interval between exposure and initiation of PEP. Once symptoms of rabies show up, it's almost always fatal. According to the Center for Disease Control, less than ten people have ever survived rabies. They were put into induced comas and received a regimen of drugs.

The PEP shots are a four dose series in conjunction with one dose of immune globulin. These shots are given on day 0, (the day the first dose is given), then on days 3, 7, and day 14.

The Center for Disease Control put out a report that can be viewed on their website. This report was made by the Advisory Committee on Immunization Practices (ACIP). The committee recently recommended the four dose series of PEP shots. The ACIP previously recommended a five dose series, the fifth dose to be given on day 28. The day 28 dose may still be given if a person's immune system is compromised by taking medication, such as an inhaled steroid for asthma, a drug that weakens the immune system, or if a patient has a weakened immune system from a disease such as HIV.

The studies resulting in the four instead of the five dose series may be read in full by going to the CDC website. On the bottom of the rabies page you'll find a link to the APIC website recommending the four dose series.

Now, about the shots. They're no longer given in the stomach. They're given in the deltoid muscle in the upper arm. These shots aren't painful like the old stomach shots. The pain is about like getting a flu shot. The immune globulin dose is given only one time, in and around the wound.

I had an encounter with a rabid javelina. It was just outside the kitchen door and was making a little noise, rattling the door. It was about 3:30 p.m. when javelinas aren't normally active. When I looked out the window, I didn't see anything. The door rattled again, and when I opened the door to see what was there, the javelina rushed in and bit me on the calf of the leg. The bite wasn't severe. It barely broke the skin because I jumped out of the way. It was hard to get the javelina outside again. When we finally did get it out, it began attacking objects in the yard. It bit a bicycle tire and other things. My son and I had to shoot it.

The Fish and Game Department had the javelina checked for rabies, and it tested positive. I underwent the rabies shots. The one-time immune globulin shot was not felt, because the area of the wound was deadened.

I found out later that two men who lived nearby had been feeding this javelina and its mate. The animals were taking food from the men's hands. It's quite possible that the one that bit me was looking for food. It had lost much of its fear of people and had come right up to the door, which isn't normal behavior for a javelina, rabid or not. The men were lucky that the animal hadn't been sick with rabies when they were hand feeding it. They would have been bitten.

RATTLESNAKES

Arizona Diamondback
Photo by Jamie Colee

Rattlesnakes are probably the most misunderstood animal on the desert. Their scientific name is *Crotalus Sistrurus*. Crotalus is from the Greek, meaning "castanet". Sistrurus is a Latinized form of the Greek word for "tail rattler".

There are many myths and misbeliefs concerning rattlesnakes. They are native to the Americas. North and South America are the only places in the world where they're found. There are 36 species of known rattlesnakes. While other states and places have larger rattlesnakes, the Sonoran Desert in Arizona has 13 species, which is more than any other place.

Since eleven of the 13 species live in the Sonoran Desert, it's imperative that we who live here and those who visit and use the desert for recreation and other uses learn to live with these amazing creatures. Phoenix is in the heart of the Sonoran Desert, and most of the people who visit and live in Arizona are around the Phoenix area.

The first step in living with rattlesnakes is to learn how they live and behave so one can avoid unpleasant contact with them.

Rattlesnakes are very complex reptiles. They are among the few animal groups with duel vision. Along with their eyes, they have sensory organs in their upper jaws that can actually see infrared images. They can detect heat from a candle at a distance of 30 feet. When a snake stalks its prey, the heat given off by the victim's body creates a heat image that's integrated into the snake's brain along with its visual image, giving the snake "heat vision" as well as reular vision. This makes the rattlesnake an excellent nocturnal predator. These heat-sensing organs are located between the eye and nostril on each side of the head and look like little pits. The rattlesnake is a viper called "pit viper".

All rattlesnakes are venomous. Their venom is a very complex toxic saliva. It consists of proteins and enzymes which start the digestive process of breaking down skin cells and tissues at the time of the bite. The venom also contains hemotoxins and anticoagulants that break down the blood and neurotoxins, which attack the nervous system. The neurotoxins are the most toxic and lethal of these, and they cause circulatory arrest and respiratory and muscular paralysis. The venom of the Mojave rattlesnake of the Mojave and Sonoran Deserts consists mostly of neurotoxins, and therefore, is the most dangerous, being considered ten times more potent than the other rattlesnakes.

The Mojave rattler can range from a brown, to a pale yellow, pink, or light green color. It can be confused with the western diamondback rattlesnake. The Mojave has a diamond pattern down its back, as does the diamondback, but the diamond pattern fades out about the last third of the length of the Mojave, and it continues to the tail on the diamondback. Both types of snakes have black and white rings on the tail above the rattles, but the white ring of the Mojave is much wider than the black ring, while on the diamondback, the rings are about the same width. Diamondbacks can grow to be much larger than the Mojave, reaching a length of five and a half feet long, while the Mojave rarely reaches a length of four feet.

Rattlesnakes use their venom to catch prey. They feed on mice, rats, small rabbits, birds, bird eggs, gophers, and any other small animal they can catch and swallow.

When a snake bites its prey it uses its fangs, which are hollow teeth. They act much like hypodermic needles. Each fang is connected to a venom gland by a venom duct. These venom glands, or sacks, are located on the upper side in the back of the snake's head. The fangs are long and curved and lie parallel to the jaws when the snake's mouth is closed. When the snake opens its mouth to bite, muscles in the jaw extend the fangs perpendicular to the jaw. Snakes shed their fangs about every 28 days. They can be found in prey animals and are passed through the snake's digestive system.

After biting the prey, the snake immediately releases it, then uses its heat sensory organs, eyes, nostrils, and forked tongue to follow the prey. There is a small organ called a Jacobson's organ located on the roof of the snake's mouth that interprets chemical scents from the forked tongue and increases the snake's ability to trail prey.

Snakes don't chew their food, but swallow it whole. Their jaws have a special joint that allows them to open their mouths very wide. The venom is for catching prey and not necessarily for defensive tactics, although this can be a very good defense. When a rattler bites for defense, about 20% of the time it doesn't inject any venom. These are called "dry bites". It's not known why the snakes elect to bite this way. Perhaps when a snake bites a person in a defensive manner, it knows that it cannot swallow a person and saves the venom for catching food.

Contrary to popular belief, rattlesnakes by nature aren't aggressive. They don't want contact with humans any more than we want contact with them. Rattlesnakes are very good at feeling vibrations in the ground and can feel when a person or a large animal like a horse, or even a dog, is walking by. They'll usually hide until it is safe for them to leave, and they do so quickly. We have observed them doing this on more than one occasion. Of course, there is always an exception, and sometimes a rattler will be somewhat aggressive. This is rare and not the usual behavior of rattlesnakes, but it's a good thing to remember if one is encountered in the desert or happens to wander into your camp or yard. Also, if a rattler is provoked or feels threatened, it is common for it to become aggressive. There are about 150 cases of snakebite in Arizona a year. Of these only 1% are fatal.

Another myth is that a rattlesnake will always give warning by rattling. Many times a rattler is trying to hide and doesn't want you to know it's there. If a rattler is suddenly surprised and feels threatened, it won't rattle, it'll just strike. Many times you won't know a rattlesnake is close by. But this isn't always the case. One time a friend and I were out and a snake started rattling when we were about 30 feet away. Another time, my mother and I were trying to get a snake to rattle because they had guests who had never heard this sound. The snake never did rattle. These situations are rather unusual, but it shows that there are no hard and fast rules governing when a snake will give warning. Another factor is that if the weather is wet, as in the monsoon season, and the rattle is wet, it won't make noise, even though the snake may be trying to get it to sound.

It's not true that you can tell a rattlesnake's age by the length or number of rattles it has. Snakes grow a new segment on their rattles every time they shed their skin. They can do this more than once a year, and sometimes several times a year, depending on the food supply and the growth rate of the particular snake. Rattles are brittle, and it's common for them to break off.

Another common belief is that rattlesnakes lay eggs. They don't. They give live birth. The baby snakes haven't developed their rattles yet. They have a small pre-button, which is the first rattle segment. The snake cannot rattle until another button, or segment, is added. This happens when the skin is shed for the first time.

The rattles are actually modified scales from the tail tip and are made of keratin, the same as human hair and fingernails. They are hollow and need at least two rattles to make noise, as they need to rub against each other in order to make sound.

Baby rattlers are doubly dangerous because they can't rattle a warning and are very poisonous. They should never be handled or treated with any less caution than adult snakes.

Rattlesnakes hibernate during the colder winter months. Here in the Sonoran Desert, snakes commonly go into hibernation in latter October or November, and they come out of hibernation in April but can come out earlier when the weather is warm. While seeing a rattler in January is somewhat unlikely, it happens. We have seen rattlesnakes out in every month of the year. It's always a good idea to be on the lookout for them anytime you're out and about. They are most active when the temperature is between 70 and 90 degrees.

Rattlesnakes can't regulate their body temperature and are affected by both heat and cold. If a snake is too cold, it will become sluggish and soon die. If a snake becomes too hot, it will also die. In the hot summer months, snakes will stay under bushes, rocks, crevasses, caves, and cracks, where it's cooler during the heat of the day. Rattlers are mostly nocturnal creatures and are most active at night during the hot summer months. During the months when the days are warm and the nights cool, as in March, and sometimes April, snakes move during daylight hours, especially in the early morning and evening.

Rattlesnakes are very adept at swimming and will be seen in the water, but are hard to see when they are there. What you will probably see at first are ripples and maybe a small wake like a stick being slowly dragged through the water. If you are up in a boat the snake may be more easily seen.

FIGURE 1: Rattlesnake

There are many varieties of snakes in the Southwest, and one snake, the bull snake, looks a lot like a rattlesnake at first glance. So how do you tell if it's a rattlesnake? One way is the distinctive shape of the head of a rattlesnake. It's shaped like a flat triangle. Note the snake in Figure 1. The tail with the rattles can't be seen, but the head gives away that it is a rattlesnake.

Figure 2 shows the head of a bull snake. It's more elongated and doesn't look so much like a flat triangle. Another thing about a bull snake is that it will emulate a rattlesnake, even to shaking its tail like a rattler.

FIGURE 2: Bull Snake

Unless you can see the head or tail of a bull snake, it's hard to tell it from a rattlesnake. If you see a snake and aren't sure what kind it is, *don't try to get close to it to see if it has rattles or a triangle head. Leave it alone!* It's not worth the risk involved to try to positively identify it.

All animals in the wild should be treated with caution and left alone to go about their daily routines. Most wild animals will shy away from human contact.

It's fairly easy to tell the other species of snakes from rattlesnakes because they are all marked differently from a rattlesnake.

TIPS FOR AVOIDING RATTLESNAKES

It has been said that to avoid rattlesnakes, you must think like a snake. The more you know about rattlers, the better you can think like one. Ask yourself if it's a day that a snake would be likely to be out and about. If it is, use extreme caution. If it's a day that's cold, and snakes aren't likely to be out, still use caution, even though you probably won't see one. There is always that "one chance in a thousand," and you don't know when that chance will turn up. All it takes is one careless second. Those of us who have lived on the desert in rural areas all of our lives always have an eye open and an ear tuned for a rattler whether we are fully conscious of it or not.

Ask yourself where you would likely be if you were a snake. We know that snakes like to stay hidden, so avoid places where they might hide, such as piles of debris, bushes, high grass, large rocks, cracks in rocks, under porches, sheds, parked cars, and such places.

We also know that snakes are sensitive to vibration in the ground, so it's a good idea to make noise when approaching places where snakes may be. Carry a walking stick, and hit the ground and rocks with it every few steps. Doing this will increase your chances that a snake will leave before you get close enough for it to strike.

If it's cool and sunny, it's common for a snake to be out in the sun in plain sight keeping warm, so watch where you're walking. I actually stepped over a snake in the desert and saw it only when I was about to step on it. The snake was stretched out full length on an old road. It was November, when snakes were supposed to be hibernating. It never moved or rattled. It just lay there while I went on my way. We have seen them out in roads, on pavement, rocks, or in the sand sunning themselves during a warm winter day.

Never reach into or under places where snakes can hide. Always use a stick, shovel, or similar tool to turn over rocks, old boxes, or poke into tall weeds from a safe distance. Use caution when entering sheds. Hit the side, rattle the door, and make other noise. This may make a rattler hiding inside start rattling.

There is a chance that a hidden snake won't rattle. After opening an unused shed, take a shovel or long stick to move some of the articles inside to make the snake move or rattle so you can see or hear it.

We've already mentioned that you should wear a good high top shoe when hiking in the desert. This is not only to protect you from rocks, brush, and cactus, but it might also protect you from snakebite. The higher and thicker the top, the better. Snakes don't typically bite high on the leg. Their prey is small, and they habitually strike close to the ground. Most of the time, they will make a defensive bite low. They are true "ankle biters". It's also a good habit not to wear shorts when hiking. Wear long trousers, as these might be some protection.

There are snake repellant sprays that you can put on yourself to repel snakes, kind of like insect repellant. We've never used these, so can't say for sure how effective they are or recommend one brand over another.

There is a snake vaccine for dogs, which we give our dogs. There is also one being developed for horses at the writing of this book.

Using these precautions will greatly increase your chances of not being the victim of a snake bite, but there is always a good chance of seeing one. If a snake is encountered, <u>never</u> try to get close to it, catch it, kill it, touch it, tease it, or in any way put yourself in danger of being bitten. They can strike the length of their body from a coiled position as well as strike when they are stretched out full length. Snakes will become aggressive and defend themselves if being threatened or provoked. If a snake is seen in the wilderness, walk away from it, and leave it alone. If a snake is encountered in your yard or a public place, call a professional to remove it. Don't try to do it yourself.

The Arizona Sonoran Museum has some interesting statistics: ninety percent of people that are bitten by snakes are trying to catch, kill, tease, or get too close to them. Eighty percent of the people that are bitten are young males. Young men are the most likely to play around with snakes. Alcohol is often a factor in these instances.

You can reduce the risk of snakes around your yard by keeping grass short so they are more easily seen. Pull weeds out, keep piles of lumber, bricks, and debris down. If you have a shed that snakes can crawl under, fix it so they can't. Discourage rabbits, mice, rats, gophers, and other small animals that snakes dine on from coming into your yard by not leaving water or food that they may eat. Having a cat or dog may discourage a snake from wandering into your yard. Again, think like a snake and ask yourself if your yard is a friendly place for a snake to reside.

WHAT IF I AM BITTEN BY A RATTLER?

If, after all you can do to prevent it, you do get bitten, <u>you must seek professional medical attention as quickly as possible.</u>

The most common rattlesnake bite is the diamondback. All rattlesnake bites are serious and painful, even though they're fatal in just 1% of bitten victims. Because rattlesnake venom attacks skin cells and breaks down blood cells, this makes healing the area around the bite very difficult and slow. If medical attention isn't given soon enough, the entire limb where the bite is may be affected. Amputations have been known to be necessary in victims who have not taken care of themselves soon enough.

Even if it was a nonpoisonous snake that bit you, medical attention is still required, as puncture wounds from fangs can become infected easily and are painful. A bite from any wild animal is serious, and medical attention is required. If it was a poisonous snake that bit you or someone with you, symptoms will show up soon enough, and medical help is already there or soon will be.

If you're bitten by a rattlesnake, you should call 911 to get emergency help on the way as soon as possible, or get the victim on the way to the hospital if you are in an out-of-the-way place. The sooner medical attention is administered, the better are the chances that the victim will recover fully and not sustain lasting damage. If your doctor or poison control center tells you to do something that isn't in this volume or is contrary to the recommendations given here, by all means follow their advice. Each situation is unique, and medical research is constantly uncovering new information and better ways to treat snakebite.

Here are some things that can be done until medical help arrives or you can get the bite victim to a hospital:

Remain calm and keep the victim calm. You can't help very much if you panic, and if you do, you'll be unable to think clearly. Also, you may cause the victim to panic.

Move the patient to a safe area. The snake might still be around. Keep the bitten area below the level of the heart if you can. If bitten on an extremity, keep it as still as possible.

Remove jewelry such as rings, watches or bracelets. Take off shoes, and loosen tight clothing from the extremity with the bite in case of swelling.

There are a number of snake bite kits on the market. If you get one, avoid getting one that has a scalpel for cutting the wound. *Never* cut a bite wound of any kind. You'll open up more blood vessels and increase the chance of spreading the poison throughout your body. You'll also increase the chance of infection. Snake fangs are curved and long, and it's unlikely that you will make an incision in the right place, anyway. You probably won't make the cut deep enough, as the snake's fangs are long.

If you know what kind of snake bit you, this will help. Don't waste time trying to find the snake or get close to it to positively identify it. This information isn't crucial. The antivenin treatment doesn't require knowing what species the rattlesnake is. People have been bitten, or bitten again, by getting too close trying to see what kind of snake bit them or their friend. Now you have two people in trouble or one person in double trouble. However, if you happen to note anything about the snake, tell the medical professionals.

Some experts recommend tying a light, restrictive band (not a tourniquet) both above and below the bite a few inches. If you do this, the bands *must not* be tied so tightly as to shut off blood circulation as it does in a tourniquet. It's very dangerous to stop blood circulation. The purpose of these bands is to restrict lymphatic flow, not blood flow. If you can't insert your forefinger under the bandage without undue force, the bands are too tight. You must keep checking the tightness of these bands because swelling will make them tighten. They must be readjusted from time to time. If you're not absolutely sure how to do this, it's better that you don't. We strongly recommend that you take a first aid course and learn the proper way to perform this procedure before you decide to use it.

Recommended by some, is to apply strong suction *without cutting*, directly on the main bite or puncture marks. If you choose this method, you have to do it within the first few seconds of the bite. It's unclear how effective suctioning is. It may help a little. Some instruction sheets in kits tell you to use it in the first 15 minutes. A lot of the venom is in the bloodstream in the first 15 seconds. Never try to suck out the poison with your mouth. Use a suction device. You can get a suction device from a commercial snakebite kit, or purchase a snake-bite suction device separately. Remember, treating snakebite is a serious thing, and one should get training from an authorized source before dealing with an emergency situation.

In summation, there are some definite "Dos" and "Do Nots" associated with treating snake bite. They are:

1. DO: Remove the victim to a safe location.

2. DO: Remove any jewelry and loosen any clothing near the bite, because it's going to swell.

3. DO: Immobilize the victim and/or bitten limb as much as possible.

4. DO: Get the victim to medical aid as soon as possible. Call 911 immediately and follow their instructions.

5. DO NOT: cut the bite. This will not work. The fangs of a snake are curved and long. You won't be able to make an incision deep enough or in the right place to be effective. You'll increase the chances of spreading the poison throughout the body by opening up more blood vessels and leave the victim susceptible to infection.

6. DO NOT: apply a tourniquet. Only a professional medical person should use a tourniquet. This is very dangerous and could result in the loss of a limb.

7. DO NOT: apply ice packs. Recent studies show that applying ice or anything cold makes the injury worse.

8. DO NOT: try to suck out the poison with your mouth. If you put your mouth on the bite, you may introduce bacteria, compounding the situation. Also, if you happen to have a cut, canker sore, cavity, or any open wound in your mouth, any venom you may get in your mouth can get into your bloodstream and make you sick as well

9. DO NOT: elevate the bite higher than the heart. The bite should be kept below the heart, if possible. This will keep the venom from spreading as fast.

10. DO NOT: run, walk fast or panic. All of these cause the heart to beat faster, spreading the poison throughout the body at a more rapid rate.

11. DO NOT: take any medication. You'll be given the proper medication and all the medication you need at the hospital by a doctor. You don't want to chance taking something that will harm you or react in a negative way to any medication that a doctor may give you.

CORAL SNAKES

Coral snakes are subdivided into two distinct groups: Old World coral snakes and New World coral snakes. We'll deal only with the New World coral snakes, of which there over 65 recognized species. Of these, this book will mostly talk about the Arizona (Micruroides euryxanthus) and Texas coral snakes (Micrurus fulvius tener) which roam the desert areas that we cover in this book.

The Arizona coral is clearly a separate species of coral snake, and there is controversy over the Texas coral being a separate species. The Arizona snakes are all relatively small, rarely reaching 18 to 20 inches long. The Texas coral snake is larger, growing to 24 inches long and longer.

Coral snakes are rare and have short, fixed fangs with a small mouth. These two factors make bites in humans fairly rare.

Coral snakes aren't aggressive and try to escape when in contact with people, adding to the rarity of bites. Coral snake bites account for less than 1% of the number of snake bites in the United States.

The coral snake is a solitary critter that comes out mostly at night, during the day after a rain, or when it's cloudy. It shies away from human contact, so it's rarely seen. It feeds on blind and black headed snakes, lizards, and other small smooth scale snakes.

Arizona coral snakes range from southern to central Arizona, southwestern New Mexico, and into Sinaloa in Western Mexico.

FIGURE 3: Coral snake with red touching yellow

Coral snakes in the southwestern desert areas have a look-alike that is harmless. This is the king snake.

There are various sayings about identifying corals, such as, "Red touch yellow, kill a fellow, red touch black, friend of Jack," or "Red touch black venom lack," or "Red on yellow you're a dead fellow, red on black, you're ok, Jack"

FIGURE 4: Coral with no yellow bands

These sayings are only partly true. There are coral snakes with no yellow on them at all. Figure 3 shows a coral snake with yellow bands touching the red bands, like in the poem. Figure 4 shows a coral snake with white bands and no yellow bands. The white bands touch the red bands and may be substituted for the yellow bands in the rhyme. Sometimes the white bands aren't as wide as in Figure 4.

FIGURE 5: Black and red coral

Figure 5 shows a coral snake with neither yellow nor white bands, just black and red bands.

So how do you identify a coral from the look-alikes? Figure 6 shows a King snake. Note that the white bands look like they're in the middle of the black bands. They don't touch the red bands. Note the head of the king snake in Figure

7. It's not all black. Note the head of the coral snake in Figure 8. It is black to just behind the eyes, as is the coral snake in figure 5.

CORAL SNAKE VENOM

FIGURE 6: King snake

The venom of a coral snake is a powerful neurotoxin similar to that of the cobra, but due to the small size of the snake, smallness of the mouth, fangs, venom gland, and the method of injecting the venom, the amount of venom injected is much less and therefore, not as dangerous as the bite of a Mojave rattlesnake. Also, the coral snake cannot inject venom forcefully, as does a pit viper. It has to chew to inject its venom. This isn't to say that coral snake bites aren't dangerous. <u>If bitten, medical attention is required as soon as possible</u>

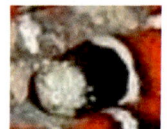
FIGURE 7: King snake

The symptoms of a bite can include nausea, vomiting and sweating. There's little to no swelling in the area of the bite. Neurological symptoms may include difficulty speaking, lethargy, or heavy eyelids. The venom from this snake most often attacks the breathing muscles, causing respiratory paralysis.

AVOIDING CORAL SNAKES

Avoiding coral snakes is much like avoiding rattlers or other desert animals that you don't want contact with. Know what their diet is, where they're likely to hide, when they're likely to be active, and be careful around these areas, especially during the times when they are most likely to be active.

Coral snakes spend the majority of their time in their burrows underground. They hide in desert scrub, grasslands, woodlands, and farmlands. According to the Arizona Sonoran Museum, they are found in levels to 5,800 feet. They can also be found in rocky areas.

Be careful when gardening. The coral snake likes damp, vegetated areas. Again, never reach into or under places where coral snakes can hide. Always use a stick or shovel or some other long tool to turn over rocks, old boxes, or poke into tall weeds from a safe distance.

FIGURE 8: Coral snake

IF BITTEN BY A CORAL SNAKE

In the rare event of a coral snake bite, *get medical attention as soon as possible.* The coral snake venom is one of the most potent in any North American snake. Although they can't inject a large amount of venom, it's still dangerous. If bitten you should call 911 immediately to get emergency help on the way as soon as possible. Keep the victim as calm as you can. Stay calm yourself. Follow the advice given to you from the 911 operator, and get to a hospital as soon as possible. As with rattlesnakes, *do not cut the bite wound.*

The "Do" and "Do Nots" if someone is bitten by a coral snake are the same as if you are bitten by a rattlesnake.

SCORPIONS

It's been estimated that there are more than 1,400 species of scorpions worldwide. There are about 90 species in the U.S., forty (almost half) of which live in Arizona. If you live in Arizona, you may not have seen what look like forty different varieties, not only because they look similar, but they aren't overly aggressive and will try to get away from you and hide.

The life span of a scorpion is about six years. It takes a little over two years for one to reach maturity. They're born live, and the mother carries them on her back from one to three weeks. The young then climb down and are on their own.

FIGURE 9: Bark scorpion

Like rattlesnakes, the best way to avoid scorpions and being stung is to learn about them. Learn where they hide, when they are most likely to be out and about, how they live, what they eat, how to recognize the most poisonous ones, and how to discourage them from coming into your living space or camp.

Scorpions are arachnids, meaning that like a spider, they have eight legs. They have an exoskeleton (external skeleton) and a pair of arms in front called pedipalps with lobster-like pincers on the end. These pincers are for holding prey and for defense. The pedipalps have various types of sensory hairs that sense different vibrations in the air and are sensitive to the touch. Scorpions have a pair of median eyes and two to five pairs of lateral eyes at their front corners. Some cave dwelling scorpions have no eyes at all, as they spend all their time in complete darkness.

All scorpions are venomous to one degree or another. There are twenty five species worldwide capable of killing healthy adult humans, but none of these are in North America.

The most venomous scorpion in North America is the bark scorpion. (Figure 9). Its sting is very painful and can cause numbness and a tingling sensation in adult humans. This can last from twenty four to seventy two hours. Because the venom can numb a hand or foot, it can cause some loss of use to that area, or even extend to an arm or a leg. It may cause a hand, foot, or limb to have convulsions. Scorpion venom has been known to cause loss of breath for a short period of time in some people.

Severity of the symptoms can depend on allergic reactions. Some people are extremely allergic. Symptoms can range from severe numbness and frothing at the mouth to paralysis and a reaction that may be confused with a seizure. It's estimated that the number of people stung by scorpions in the southwest numbers in the thousands annually. But despite some severe reactions, fatalities are very rare and are limited to small children and adults who aren't in good health. There have been only four recorded fatalities from scorpions since 2001.

The appearance of the bark scorpion is somewhat different from other varieties. It is small, usually less than 3 inches long. It's a solid yellow to straw color with no black on its back. Most other kinds of scorpions display a black or dark colored back. The entire body of the bark scorpion is more slender than other varieties, especially the tail. Note the tail and body on the bark scorpion in Figure 10. It's much narrower than other varieties. Note the tail and body on the striped tail scorpion in Figure 11 and the tails and bodies in subsequent photos.

FIGURE 10: Bark scorpion

The scorpion's "tail" is actually a part of the abdomen. The abdomen is called the metasoma. The tail always has five segments, not including the venom sack. At the very end of the tail, or metasomal segments, is a bulb shaped segment that contains the venom glands and the venom. This "venom sack" is called the telson and contains a sharp, curved stinger on the end for delivering the venom. Figure 12 shows the "business end" of a scorpion's tail.

FIGURE 11: Striped Tail Scorpion

FIGURE 12: Tail with the Telson and stinger

The largest scorpion on the desert is the giant desert hairy scorpion. (See Figure 13) It can reach a length of five inches and is a fearsome looking creature. Despite its looks, its sting is not very venomous, but it can be painful. The desert hairy scorpion usually lives in low sandy areas and is also sometimes known as the desert sand scorpion.

Scorpions are mostly nocturnal, but can also be active in daytime hours when the days are cool, and especially after rains. They are always in search of water and can live on only water for two weeks or more.

Scorpions are masterful at hiding and have many hiding places. They are able to blend in with their surroundings and are very hard to see, even when looking for them.

FIGURE 13: Photo by Wendy Jones

All scorpions like to hide under things. They'll hide under almost anything. They can be found under wood piles, boards, the bark of old stumps, dead branches, and in the case of the bark scorpion, (which is one of the few species of scorpions that can climb) they can also be found in live trees. Scorpions lurk under rocks, bushes, in holes, cracks and crevasses in cement, porches, boxes, and any appliance that is outdoors. If there are any cans, plastic bags, pieces of cardboard or other debris lying around, this is a good place to find a scorpion. In general, if something is on the ground or on a shelf where a scorpion can hide, you can be sure that sooner or later there will be one there, especially if the area is moist or it's a place where there are a lot of insects, such as an outdoor area with a night light. Night lights really attract these nighttime pests.

While scorpions shy away from people, they'll live in close proximity with us. When camping in the desert or sleeping outdoors, it's always wise to shake out your shoes before putting them on. Not only do scorpions like to crawl into a pair of vacant shoes, so do a lot of other small desert dwellers.

FIGURE 14: Giant desert scorpion ready for action

When camping, if you don't have a good tent that is bug proof, scorpions can also be hiding under clothing, sleeping bags, or blankets. You should shake these out before using them.

Scorpions will get into your house, especially if you live in an outlying area or in an area of new construction. Their habitat has been disturbed, and their natural hiding places have been taken away. They'll be found anywhere in the house they can hide. They'll be in clothing drawers, under clothing, under living room furniture such as couches and recliners, and you may find them in closets. They'll most often be found in sinks, bathtubs, showers and toilet areas, where there is moisture. They'll get into your shoes and clothing on the floor in areas where you find a lot of scorpions. For this reason, we not only shake our shoes when camping, but indoors as well.

Deserts aren't the only places you have to watch for scorpions. They have a wide range of habitats. They live in grasslands, deciduous forests, pine forests, and rain forests. They have even been found under rocks in the snow at elevations over 12,000 feet in the Himalayan Mountains. They are certainly all over the southwest, in our pine forests and high country as well as the desert.

An interesting thing about scorpions is that they are fluorescent. That is, they will glow when an ultra violet light, or black light, is shown on them at night. Figure 15 shows a scorpion caught under a UV light. They actually show up more of a green color than a photo will show, and they really glow.

AVOIDING SCORPIONS

When camping, select a place that's as free of large rocks, brush, sticks and other desert debris as possible.

FIGURE 15: Scorpion under UV light

Have a good tent that has a high snake band in the door opening and keep it closed at all times. Bring camp chairs to sit on. If you sit on a stump or large rock, make sure that it's free of any cracks and holes and that there is no debris nearby that a scorpion could crawl out from under and onto you. Sit well away from the woodpile if you have a campfire. When picking up firewood, wear gloves. Check to see no scorpions are under it or in any loose bark on the wood. When turning over rocks or anything that a scorpion can hide under, do so with a stick or some other long object. When folding up your tent, make sure no scorpion is hiding under it.

Around your home, the first step in avoiding scorpions and other pests is to have your house and surrounding area sprayed with an insecticide. This will help, but scorpions are hard to control with insecticides alone. Insecticides will also keep away small insects and bugs that scorpions eat. This is important because if you take away their food source from an area, there is less of a motive for them to live there.

Another method that can be used to keep away scorpions and pests is to remove anything in the yard around the house that they can hide under, such as trash, logs, lumber, bricks, boxes and other loose items.

In desert areas, natural landscaping is often used because of the lack of water in the southwest. If your yard has desert landscaping, large landscaping rocks should be kept a distance from the house and walkways.

Scorpions like shrubbery. Keep it away from the house and walkways as well. Keep shrubs trimmed so they don't hang over on the ground. Any flower beds shouldn't be against the house. Flowers need water, and this is an ideal place for scorpions. They'll certainly find their way into your house should they decide to make their home in these moist areas. Not only do flower beds provide needed moisture, but they bring insects that scorpions love to dine on.

All living things need water. Water is very scarce on the desert, and where there is water you'll find all manner of desert critters So, please take proper precautions. Keep a sharp lookout and wear protective clothing such as gloves and sturdy shoes when tending your yard.

If you have a lawn, keep it mowed short, especially near the house. Keep ground cover plants away from the house, and minimize the area devoted to ground cover plants.

Store garbage containers away from the house. Check under them when they are moved.

If you have a fireplace, store the firewood as far from the house as possible and always use gloves when bringing it inside. Check each piece before bringing it in. Do this carefully, as bark scorpions hide under the dry, loose bark.

Install tight weather stripping around doors and windows. Scorpions can squeeze through a small crack, so pay particular attention to any space under doors. This is where a lot of scorpions enter your house. Keep screens and windows in good repair

Calk around pipes and other openings in walls. Repair any cracks in stucco walls and board sidings.

Be careful around sinks and bath tubs. We live in a rural area, and we are careful how we remove any dishes that have been sitting in the kitchen sink.

Always be careful where you are reaching and putting your hands when outdoors. If you have to pick up a rock, board, pail, or other object in the yard, roll it over or move it first with a stick, shovel, or some other instrument from a safe distance. Gloves should always be worn.

Scorpions are very fast little creatures. It's best to keep this in mind whenever you encounter one. They can use their stinger faster than you can see it move and can turn around and sting faster than you can move your hand out of the way. As with all critters, if you encounter a scorpion out where people are not likely to be around for a while, and you're not staying around the area, it's best to leave it alone.

Again, be careful where you are sitting when you're camping, hiking or in the yard. Large rocks, boxes, stumps, or old chairs should always be examined before sitting on them. We've been with more than one person who was stung on the rear end or upper leg when sitting on a log or large rock without first checking it out. We took one man who sat on a scorpion quite a few miles out of the desert to a doctor. It took more than two hours to get him there. The doctor told the man that if he wasn't having a severe reaction of some kind by that time, he most likely wouldn't have any. He explained that the sting was in the fatty tissue of his rear end, wouldn't spread throughout the body very fast, and he would metabolize the poison as fast as it spread. He told the man that if it would make him feel better, he could go home and sit in a basin of ice water. I can't imagine that making anyone feel better, but that's what he did.

All of these precautions may seem ridiculous, but thousands of people are stung throughout the United States each year. Some of these incidents could have been prevented if a little more caution had been used.

WHAT TO DO IF STUNG BY A SCORPION

Of course, all stings can't be prevented, and there are some things that can be done in the event of scorpion sting.

The first thing to do if stung by a scorpion is to call your doctor and/or your local poison control center, and follow their advice. You should to go to a hospital, doctor or clinic if you are experiencing involuntary eye movement, blurred vision, difficulty breathing, tingling sensations, impaired speech, twitching muscles, drooling, or hyperactivity. These may indicate severe allergic reactions to scorpion venom or especially, a bark scorpion sting.

You can wash the area with soap and cool water. Avoid hot water, as it may warm the sting area and help spread the venom. You must remain as calm as you can. Keep the extremity with the sting as still as possible, and keep the area of the sting below heart level. According to the Arizona Poison Control Center, you shouldn't apply ice, but you should apply a cool compress.

If the victim is very young or very elderly, get them to a medical facility as soon as possible. Don't spend time applying first aid. It's more important to get them to a hospital or other emergency facility where they can get the necessary medication, such as antivenin and pain killers. Most scorpion stings won't require hospitalization, but don't wait for severe symptoms before going to the hospital. It's better to be safe, and get treatment. The things to do and not to do for a scorpion sting are much the same as for snake bite. You can follow the same rules.

BLACK WIDOW SPIDERS

There are many species of spiders living in our deserts, and you will encounter a lot of them. However, there are only two types in southwestern desert areas that are dangerous to humans. They are the black widow spider and Arizona brown spider.

Black widow spiders inhabit most of the warmer regions of the world and are found in all four deserts of the American Southwest. They can differ in appearance slightly. The species of black widow spider most likely encountered is the *Latrodectus Hesperus*. The female is the most dangerous and can be recognized by her shiny black appearance and bright red hourglass marking on the underside of her abdomen. (Figure 16). This red marking is easy to see because the black widow most often hangs upside down in her web. Sometimes the red marking isn't in the shape of an hour glass. Occasionally, just red spots are displayed or markings that look like two triangles. Black widows displaying no red marks have been found. Any shiny black spider with red markings is a species of female black widow.

FIGURE 16: Black widow

The male is a lighter color, about half the size of the female (Figure 17) and has longer legs in proportion to the female. The hour glass marking can be seen, but isn't as defined. He can have stripes or markings on the upper side of his back.

Con0trary to popular belief, the female doesn't always kill and eat the male after mating. This is actually the exception rather than the rule. Males can sometimes escape the female even when she is trying to kill him.

Black widows aren't the only spiders to cannibalize their mates. This isn't all that uncommon in the spider world. Wolf spiders sometimes eat each other. The female will eat an older male, and a male will eat an older female.

The black widow is the most venomous spider in North America. Its venom is reputed to be more potent than the Mojave rattlesnake. Despite this, fatalities from black widow bites are few. Less than 1% of victims die. As with other poisonous bugs in Arizona and southwestern deserts, small children and elderly adults, adults in poor health, those who have very high blood pressure or heart disease are most at risk.

The venom of the black widow spider is a neurotoxin, which attacks the nervous system and is the most dangerous of the venoms. Although a black widow bite is potentially lethal, it's seldom fatal because of the small amount of venom she's able to inject.

The male black widow is considerably smaller than the female and isn't known to bite humans, so isn't considered dangerous. Even if it did bite, it can inject such a small amount of venom that it probably wouldn't be much of a health threat. The venom glands of a male black widow are much smaller in proportion than female.

Baby black widows hatch out of eggs, which are contained in a case made from spider web spun by the female. (Figure 18) She can produce from four to nine egg cases in a summer. Each case contains from 100 to 300 or more eggs.

When born, the spiderlings are white to yellowish-white and are harmless to humans. Many of these young spiders don't survive because of cannibalism or lack of food or proper shelter. They gradually turn black and acquire the red hour glass

Figure 18: Male Black Widow

marking each time they molt and become more mature. It takes from two to four months for them to become mature enough to breed.

The spiderlings disperse from their web by a process known as "ballooning". They do this by extruding silk threads and letting the air currents catch them, carrying them off to parts unknown.

Black widows are cobweb builders. Their webs, which are most often built near the ground, have no discernable pattern and can be as large as a foot across. There is a dense area of silk to one side of them that serves as the spider's daytime hideaway. The webs trap the spider's food, which includes insects, cockroaches, beetles, other spiders, and any small bug that happens to wander in. The webs can be found in places like woodpiles, under vehicles that have been parked for a time, such as a motor home, under trailers, in hollow stumps, thick shrubbery, sheds, rodent burrows, crevices in large rocks, rubble piles, brick and stone walls, and any other place that is low, cool, hollow, hidden, or undisturbed.

Black widows won't typically build webs and live in an inhabited house. When they do, it's usually in a dark, unused corner of a basement, attic or a storeroom that isn't entered often. They may hide behind large furniture such as a dresser that isn't moved very often. Sometimes they may be found in a clothing drawer or closet that hasn't been opened for a time. It is always a good idea to shake out any clothing from these areas before putting it on.

Black widows are really shy critters and won't bite unless guarding an egg case or if they are accidentally or otherwise touched or disturbed in some manner.

BLACK WIDOW SPIDER CONTROL

To control black widow spiders, spray with an insecticide any area where a web is likely to be. This will also help eliminate the spider's food source. As with scorpions, spraying alone won't completely eliminate black widows. You'll also need to keep any fire wood, stacks of lumber, bricks, and stones away from the house, and check them often for webs, being sure to include these as well as stone and brick walls when spraying.

Since black widows rarely leave their webs, search the places where webs are likely to be found and destroy them. When a web is found, come back at night when the spider is out so you can be sure to get the spider along with the web.

Keep shrubs trimmed so they don't hang over on the ground. Keep hedges trimmed and check under and in them for webs. If you have any cactus skeletons or pieces of cactus skeletons for landscape in your yard, check these carefully because this is their natural habitat. When you're in the desert, avoid poking around in dead cacti.

Although black widows don't usually live in an inhabited house, it's a good idea to check areas that aren't entered often. Storerooms, attics, basements, sheds, and stored cardboard boxes should also be checked periodically.

IF BITTEN BY A BLACK WIDOW SPIDER

As soon as you suspect a black widow bite, try to remain calm. Do not panic, walk fast or run. Call your doctor, local poison control center, or hospital immediately. Do not apply a tourniquet. Keep the bite site below the heart if possible. Keep the extremity with the bite as immobile as possible. If bitten on the body, minimize your movements and move slowly. You can wash the bite site with cool water and soap. Apply a cool compress rather than an ice pack. Don't take any medication until advised to do so by a professional medical person. Call your doctor and/or the local poison control center. Follow their advice.

Most often, a bite from a black widow will go unnoticed for a period of time. It may feel like a pin prick, a slight scratch, or you may not feel it at all. In many cases, the spider is never found, and when symptoms show up it's sometimes hard to tell what caused them.

Symptoms from black widow bites usually start to show within twenty minutes to an hour after the bite. The first symptom is pain at the site of the bite. Some people are more allergic than others, so the pain experienced can vary from mild to severe and is generally more severe than mild. There is usually minimal swelling in the area of the bite. It may turn red, and two small puncture wounds may be visible.

Next, muscle cramps, sometimes severe, often show up. These cramps may be localized in the area of the bite, or most likely, there will be general all over cramping. Large muscle groups in the shoulder and back will especially be affected. It may also cause severe abdominal pain, weakness, or convulsions in the extremity that was bitten.

Blood pressure and heart rate may be elevated. If a victim has hypertension, this can be dangerous. Swelling of the eye lids may also occur, and the victim may become sleepy. In severe cases, vomiting, nausea, fainting, dizziness, and even chest pain, may occur. The severity of the reaction depends on the age, physical condition and allergic reaction of the person being bitten.

Black widow bites should always be treated as serious. Seek medical attention as soon as possible because you don't know what kind of a reaction you might have. If you don't see a doctor, you most likely won't die. But if you do see a doctor, you may save yourself a lot of suffering if reactions are severe. Most people experience quite a bit of pain, especially in the back and abdominal areas. A doctor can administer medication to help with pain, nausea, and other symptoms. You may also be given an antibiotic to prevent infection. Bite symptoms can last a long time, up to two weeks or more in a lot of people. Getting medical attention is essential.

ARIZONA BROWN AND BROWN RECLUSE SPIDERS

The brown recluse spider, *Loxosceles Reclusa,* (lox-sos-a-leez) is native to the southern and midwestern states and ranges as far as Georgia to the Gulf of Mexico. It is recognized by the violin shaped marking on the body, with the neck of the violin pointing toward the back of the spider. It's also known as the violin, or fiddle back spider.

FIGURE 19: Brown Recluse

As mentioned, *Loxoceles Reclusa* isn't native to Arizona, New Mexico, California, or Colorado. The only true recluse spiders found in these areas have been brought there in luggage and other ways. When they're introduced to these areas, they don't last long. For some reason, they can't survive in any locale where they aren't native.

In Arizona, however, reside several species of *Loxosceles* spiders relative to the brown recluse known as Arizona brown spiders. They also have violin shaped markings on their cephalothorax which are not quite as defined as on the recluse.

The Arizona brown spiders closely resemble the recluse. Their scientific names are *Loxosceles Arizonica, Loxosceles Apachea, Loxosceles Deserta, Loxosceles Kaiba, and Loxosceles Sabina.* They reside mostly in southern Arizona and are most prevalent around the Tucson area, ranging into central Arizona. If the legs are included, they are about the size of a nickel or a little larger. It's suspected that some of these species are more venomous than others. They all produce a bite that destroys skin tissue and is dangerous.

FIGURE 20: Arizona brown spider

Unlike most spiders, which have eight eyes, the Loxoceles group have six eyes arranged in three pairs. There is one median pair and two lateral pairs. You would need high magnification to see them, so it would be difficult to "look him in the eyes" for identification purposes.

BROWN SPIDER VENOM

The venom of the recluse and Arizona brown spider is mostly a hemotoxin, which causes a breakdown of skin, fat, and blood vessel tissue. This breakdown is called necrosis and initially begins in the area of the bite, but keeps spreading. Because of this, these spiders are sometimes called "necrotizing spiders," along with their other names.

Like the black widow, the recluse builds its webs in places like wood piles, dead wood or dead cacti in the desert, in dry washes, sheds, garages, piles of rocks, bricks, and other places that are dry and undisturbed. They will get into your house and hide in places such as attics, basements, closets and in clothing drawers that haven't been used for some time. They like to hide in bed sheets, particularly in spare bedrooms and guest rooms that haven't been recently occupied. If the beds are made up, they should always be checked carefully before anyone sleeps in them. It's best to take them apart, and make them again after checking the bedding.

Violin shaped marking

Be especially careful around any cardboard box that has been stored or unmoved for a period of time. The brown spider favors cardboard if it can find some in a quiet, unused place. A possible reason is that maybe cardboard is similar to the rotting tree bark that is their natural habitat. They also inhabit vacant shoes like many other desert creatures.

Arizona brown spiders are non-aggressive and are loners, but they seem to live around humans more than black widows do. They are found in inhabited homes more often. Like the black widow, they bite only when disturbed, as in rolling on them in bed, when they are in your clothing, or when accidentally touched.

Arizona brown spiders, like black widows, are nocturnal and are mostly active at night, but can be active in daylight hours also, if conditions warrant.

BROWN SPIDER CONTROL

The control of Arizona brown spiders is much the same as black widow control, so please refer to the section on black widow control for instructions on how to deal with these critters.

IF BITTEN BY AN ARIZONA BROWN SPIDER

As with black widow bites, brown spider bites may go unnoticed for a period of time. The bite may cause a mild stinging sensation, if noticed at all. The first symptoms may appear as long as several hours after the bite. A small white area may appear surrounded by a larger area of redness. This may have an itching pain.

Next, a blister often appears with mild swelling along with the redness. A lesion appears that looks like a bull's eye or a target. This lesion becomes an extensive, open, spreading sore as tissue is destroyed. There may be fever, chills, nausea, pain in the joints, hives, and a severe rash may develop. Unless it's a severe bite, most bites are minor with little necrosis.

If you suspect that you have been bitten by a brown spider, *it is essential to seek medical attention as soon as possible*. Although the bite may not be serious, a brown spider bite should be considered a serious medical condition. If the bite becomes necrotic, it will be very hard to treat. These bites are non-healing. There is no first aid and no antivenin for them. If left untreated, it may be necessary to amputate part or all of a limb. Even with rapid treatment, surgery may be needed to cut out dead tissue and may result in having to have skin grafts. If rapid treatment isn't administered, the sore may leave permanent damage and scarring.

Treatments that have been used and have had varying degrees of success are hyperbaric oxygen therapy (100% oxygen in a pressure chamber), dapsone, antihistamines, dextran, and others. None of these treatments have been used in controlled trials to conclusively show any benefits they may have.

As with black widow spiders, if you're bitten and don't see a doctor, you most likely won't die, but may suffer a lot of pain. You may have ugly scars or even eventually lose part or all of a limb, hand, or fingers. Seek medical attention as soon as possible.

TARANTULA SPIDERS

Before we leave spiders, there is one more that should be mentioned, and that is the North American tarantula. We mention them, not because they are overly venomous, but because they are easily confused with the more venomous species of tarantula in other parts of the world. It should be understood that the venom from the tarantulas that roam the southwestern deserts and other parts of North America are not harmful to humans, but when these large spiders (leg span can be 6 inches or more) are encountered on the desert, they can be very scary. In addition to being large, they are hairy, making them even more ferocious looking.

FIGURE 21: Tarantula

While all tarantulas around the world are venomous, only a few species are known to be harmful to humans. Contrary to popular belief, the bite from the most venomous species isn't fatal, but it can cause extreme discomfort for several days and in some rare cases hallucinations. There has never been a recorded death from a tarantula spider bite.

The dreaded "banana spider", sometimes called the banana tarantula, is actually a Brazilian wandering spider, not a tarantula. It's a completely different species (*Phoneutria*, meaning murderess) and inhabits Central and South America and is only seen in North America if one happens to be in a crate of bananas from South America. It is indeed very venomous. It can kill a human. It's a large spider similar in appearance and easily confused with the tarantula. The phoneutria has a very potent neurotoxin venom.

Desert tarantulas belong to the family *theraphosidae*. They shouldn't be harmed in any way. Despite their appearance, these spiders are very docile critters. They will only bite when being severely provoked. The greatest danger from being bitten is from infection. These tarantula have rather large, long fangs and can inflict painful puncture wounds that are hard to clean and get antibacterial medication into.

The tiny hairs on the abdomen, called urticating hairs, are also slightly venomous. When threatened, the tarantula can rub these hairs off by using its back legs. In some people, these hairs may be irritating if they get into the nose or eyes and can also irritate the skin.

The tarantula isn't often seen on the desert because this solitary creature lives in burrows in the ground, crevices in rocks, hollow logs, and tree roots. It seldom comes out of its burrow. When it does emerge, it's mostly at night to hunt, as it's a nocturnal predator. The tarantula feeds on grasshoppers, lizards, scorpions, beetles, other spiders, and various insects. It also captures small mice and other rodents. In winter, it won't actively hunt. It stores fat in its body for times of inactivity.

The tarantula lines its burrow with silk that extends to the surface. The spider is very sensitive to vibrations that are felt whenever small insects and other prey come close enough to disturb the silk. It can get out of its burrow very quickly to capture its dinner.

TARANTULA HAWK

There is a type of wasp called the "tarantula hawk" that preys on the tarantula. These large spider wasps are very colorful with their shiny blue-black bodies and bright orange wings. They are about two inches long or longer and are among the largest wasps.

Tarantula Hawk

The female tarantula hawk hunts tarantulas and uses them as food for its larvae. Her sting paralyzes the tarantula. She then drags the spider to her burrow and lays a single egg on its body. The young wasp feeds on the tarantula for several weeks until it becomes an adult. It then emerges from the burrow to carry on the cycle.

The male tarantula hawk doesn't hunt, but feeds on the flowers of milkweed, mesquite, and other flowering plants. When the fruits become fermented, the tarantula hawk will become so intoxicated that it can't fly straight. Kind of staggering in flight, you might say.

Tarantula hawks are most active in the daytime summer months, hunting the tarantula in their burrows or feeding on flowers. They avoid being out in the hottest part of the summer day.

Unlike other wasps, tarantula hawks are solitary creatures like the spiders they hunt. They aren't aggressive and won't sting without provocation. When they do, however, their sting is very painful. According to one researcher, the pain is "immediate, excruciating pain that simply shuts down one's ability to do anything, except, perhaps, scream." If you should see one, definitely leave it alone to go about its business. The tarantula hawk isn't hunting humans and isn't dangerous unless molested.

One may be observed from a little distance without getting close or disturbing it.

GILA MONSTERS

Gila monsters (pronounced hee-lah) are large, venomous lizards with teeth and a huge fat tail. They can grow 14 to 18 inches or more in length and are pink to light red with black bands or a black reticulated pattern and have a black snout. Their skin is rough and looks beaded.

Gila monsters are native to the southwestern United States and are found in Arizona, parts of California, Nevada, New Mexico, and Southwestern Utah. They range into Northwestern Mexico.

The Gila monster (Heloderma suspectum) gets its name from the Gila River Basin of Arizona, where it was once plentiful. There is a similar venomous lizard in Mexico known as the Mexican beaded lizard. These two lizards are the only two venomous lizards in the world.

Figure 22: Gila Monster

The Gila monster is not really a monster. The only way these lizards are monsters, is that they are big for a lizard. They are not aggressive, but they can seem so in order to scare off a potential enemy. This huge lizard does this by opening its mouth very wide and loudly hissing. This is usually scary to anyone witnessing this behavior. The Gila monster can take a stance that looks as if it will jump right at you. If this fails, it will turn and lumber away as fast as it can go. If it can't run, it will turn aggressive and bite if molested.

Gila monsters usually display a sluggish nature and appear to move along in no particular hurry. They have a lumbering, side to side, swinging gait when they walk. They can't run as fast as the smaller common desert lizards, and this leads many people to believe that they can't move fast. However, they're capable of moving very quickly when catching prey and can also turn 180 degrees very rapidly. If disturbed, they can move quickly to get out of the way, or on rare occasions, turn and bite. Never pick one up. They can turn and bite faster than you can move your hand out of the way.

Although their favorite, and main diet, is bird eggs, Gila monsters also eat small birds, lizards, frogs, mice, other small animals, and even baby rabbits on occasion. Catching this kind of prey requires quick motion.

They are also able to climb trees and cacti in search of eggs. Figure 23 shows a Gila monster's long toes and claws that aid in climbing. An interesting thing is that the Gila monster may only eat five or six times in a whole year. Fat is stored in the tail and abdomen for future use.

Gila monsters aren't encountered on the desert very often due to their diminishing numbers, solitary habits, and the fact that they spend most of their time in underground burrows and are mostly nocturnal in the summer months. They are most active in the spring when their food is most abundant and the weather is favorable. In the spring they are active in both daytime and nighttime. They hibernate in the winter as do rattlesnakes, and like rattlesnakes, may be out and about sunning themselves or in search of food during warmer winter days.

FIGURE 23: Toes and long claws of the gila monster

GILA MONSTER VENOM

The venom of the Gila monster is a neurotoxin. The venom gland is in the lower jaw instead of the upper jaw like a venomous snake.

The lizard doesn't have the proper musculature to forcibly inject its venom. It's instead delivered by a chewing action. This means that the Gila monster will hold onto its prey for a time in order to inject the venom. Because it can't forcibly inject venom, and its teeth are set far back in its mouth, only some of it gets into the prey. Sometimes it will turn upside down when biting a prey animal. This may help the injection process.

Although the Gila monster's venom is a potent neurotoxin, it's seldom fatal to humans. It's delivered through grooves in the hollow teeth. There have been no confirmed deaths form a Gila monster bite since 1939. Some of the reports of death from bites before that time are suspect due to primitive treatments or infections resulting from the deep punctures caused by the unclean teeth of the Gila monster. Due to the bacteria on the teeth of this lizard, infection is a real threat.

MYTHS ABOUT GILA MONSTERS

The tendency of the Gila monster to hold on while biting has given rise to the myth that when one bites, it won't let go until sunset.

Another myth is that Gila monsters can spit deadly poison. The truth is that they will hiss loudly but will not spit, especially not poison.

One story goes that the breath of a Gila monster is poisonous. This is not so, either. The source of this fable probably got its start because the Gila monster is reputed to have bad breath. If you are close enough to smell its breath, you are way too close. You need to back away from the Gila monster.

Another myth is that Gila monsters lack an anal opening and regurgitate their waste through their mouth. This also may have gotten its start because of its bad breath.

Yet another erroneous belief states that the Gila monster can jump several feet into the air in order to attack people. Although it will strike a pose that makes it look as if it will jump at you, this is a defensive tactic and it will not actually jump. It only assumes this position if it feels really threatened. Mostly, it runs away to hide.

Another fable is that Gila monsters can't move quickly. They may not be able to run in a straight line very fast, but they can move side to side very quickly in order to catch prey and bite any enemies.

The Tohono O'dham and Pima Indians believed the Gila monster possessed a spiritual power that could cause sickness, while the Seri and Yaqui Indians believed its hide had healing properties.

IF BITTEN BY A GILA MONSTER

If a Gila monster bites you, it will hold on in order to inject as much venom as it can. Your immediate problem is to remove it as quickly as possible before very much venom enters your body.

The jaws of this lizard are very strong, and it will take something like a screwdriver to pry them open. If you have a utility knife that has a screwdriver blade on it and you can get to it, do it as quickly as you can, or have someone else with you help you. If you have a pocket knife or some other knife without a screwdriver blade, it must have a very strong blade in order to pry the jaws open. Some people have even cut off a Gila monster's head to free themselves. This is very difficult, may take some time, and should be done only as a last resort. It is easier to pry the jaws open. Try this first.

As with any wild animal bite, <u>*seek medical attention as soon as possible.*</u> The bite of a Gila monster should be treated as very serious. Call 911 to get medical help on the way as soon as you can, or get the victim started to the hospital if you are in an out-of-the-way place. As in any poisonous bite, keep the victim as calm as possible, keep the bite area lower than the heart if possible, and follow the "Dos and Do Nots" in the previous sections addressing snake bites.

OTHER FACTS AND INFORMATION

The number of Gila monsters appears to be diminishing. This is partially due to urban sprawl. With cities growing and pushing into its habitat, they're forced to go into areas where they normally don't live. They're protected by Arizona and Nevada state law. It's unlawful to harass, pursue, hunt, or otherwise harm a Gila monster.

There is no reason to be afraid of a Gila monster if one is encountered. It will not attack or bite unless it's molested or feels threatened. If one is found, it may be observed from some little distance without danger. Keep in mind that these, like all desert animals, are part of the desert environment and have their place in the natural order of things. Stay at a distance, and don't be fooled into thinking that these lizards cannot turn and bite very quickly if they feel threatened.

If you encounter one of these endangered lizards in your yard or camping area, don't try to move it yourself. Contact your local authorities, such as a fire department, Game and Fish, or Animal

CENTIPEDES

FIGURE 24: Giant desert centipede

There is another creepy, crawly, slightly venomous thing in desert areas that you need to be aware of. This is a long, many legged thing called a centipede. Centipede means one hundred feet, although most of them do not have a hundred feet, or legs. One that has twenty five pairs of legs is a lot of legs for a centipede. They always have uneven pairs of legs.

There are two principle types of centipedes living in the southwestern deserts of the U.S. One is the giant desert centipede *(Scolopendra heros)* shown in Figure 24, and the other is the common desert centipede *(Scolopendra polymorpha)* shown in figure 25.

Centipedes can be identified by their wide, flat bodies and one pair of legs per segment. The giant centipede reaches a length of six to eight inches, although longer ones have been found.

The giant centipede is orange to red, with a black head and a black tail. In some locations, it has a red head and tail and is called "red headed giant centipede". The common desert centipede is somewhat smaller, about 4 to 5 inches long.

Centipedes are carnivorous and eat such things as insects, lizards, small frogs, and rodents. They are in turn eaten by owls, ringtail cats, coyotes, bobcats, and badgers.

Centipedes have a very interesting defensive mechanism. They have a pseudo head at the tail that looks like the real head. They can even run backwards as fast as forward, so it's hard for a predator to tell if it is biting the head or tail. They have a pair of modified legs on the tail that look like the antennae on the head. They are very fast moving, as one may expect from anything with 40 legs, and are very agile.

FIGURE 25: Common desert centipede

Centipedes are nocturnal creatures. Because of their nocturnal habits, they are not often seen unless they are uncovered in the daytime when you're moving debris where they are hiding.

All centipedes have poor eyesight, even though many varieties have compound eyes. They track their prey through the sense of touch.

CENTIPEDE VENOM

Although centipedes are venomous, their bite isn't considered dangerous to healthy adults. However, it may be dangerous to the elderly, infirm, children, or those allergic to the venom as in a bee sting allergy, which can be dangerous and may cause anaphylactic shock. The bite of a centipede is, however, very painful. The pain can last for several hours, or even up to two days. In severe cases, the victim may experience fever and chills. The bitten area can swell for several days, and even after the swelling subsides, it may reoccur for several weeks.

The centipede uses a pair of gnathosomes, or gastropods, also known as maxillipeds, to inject venom into its prey. The gnathosomes are pincerlike appendages in front of the legs, so the bite is actually a pinch instead of an actual bite.

In addition to a painful bite, the centipede's legs have a sharp, clawlike ending that can dig into the skin if one crawls over you. They don't normally grab on with the claws unless they're disturbed in some way. If the claws penetrate the skin, this may result in an infection, which is hard to get rid of. It can leave scars that look like the graph at the right. :::::::: We have seen a few people with such scars, although this isn't very common.

AVOIDING CENTIPEDES

Avoiding centipedes is much the same as avoiding scorpions, as centipedes hide in many of the same places and have much the same diet as scorpions.

IF BITTEN BY A CENTIPEDE

As with any bite, seek medical attention as soon as possible. It is important to stay as calm as possible. Remember that centipede bites aren't very serious in a healthy adult. Because the bite is very painful and the venom injected isn't usually very dangerous, pain control is going to be a lot of the treatment. A centipede bite victim may be given antihistamines.

The pain will subside in a few hours to a couple of days, but the wound will take longer to heal because the bite is mildly necrotic, like a brown spider bite or rattlesnake bite, but much less so. The necrotic tissue safely heals in a week or so with no lasting effects.

You should wash the infected area with soap and cold water. After the infected area is washed, a hot compress may be applied. Some studies suggest this may ease the pain somewhat.

AFRICANIZED BEES

WHAT THEY ARE

Africanized bees are honey bees from Africa (Apis Mellefera) that are very aggressive in protecting their domain. They attack in mass with no seeming provocation and have been known to follow any perceived threat great distances, sometimes continuing pursuit up to a quarter of a mile or more.

The ancestors of the Africanized honey bee live throughout Europe and Africa south of the Sahara Desert.

A large African honey bee colony may contain as many as 2,000 soldier bees ready to attack or defend anything they perceive as a threat.

By contrast, the regular, or European, honey bee typically has 200 soldier bees guarding the hive. Africanized bees react much quicker, attack in greater numbers, and as mentioned, pursue their quarry longer distances.

HOW THEY GOT HERE

Honey bees are not native to the Western Hemisphere. Europeans brought them to the U. S. and South America around 400 years ago. However, they didn't do well in the tropics of South America, so the aggressive African honey bee was brought to Brazil in 1956, in the hope of creating a honey bee better suited to tropical conditions.

These African bees escaped before a gentler strain of bee was developed. They bred with the wild bees and domesticated honey bees. The African bees killed the queen in the domestic hive and established their own queen. This new hybrid took on the characteristics of the African bee and lost many of the traits of the domestic honey bee. They became known as "Africanized bees," or "killer bees," because of their tendency to readily attack humans and animals.

WHEN THEY REACHED THE UNITED STATES

In 1990, just outside the small town of Hidalgo in south Texas, a swarm of honey bees was identified as Africanized. They had officially arrived in the U.S.

HOW FAST THEY ARE SPREADING

Africanized bees spread about 200 miles a year. They can do this because they can increase the population of their colonies very quickly, and they swarm often. They literally live on the move and are now found throughout the southwestern U.S. They range through southern California, Arizona, Nevada, southern Utah, southern New Mexico, southwest Texas, and have spread eastward into Louisiana, southern Georgia, Tennessee, and southern Florida. No one can tell how far they will spread or how far north they will eventually go, but they are found farther north each year.

Rainfall, available flora, and food sources also determine the rate of the spread of Africanized bees. They're very adaptable and survive even thrive in harsh and unpredictable conditions.

If food is scarce, Africanized bees can move their entire colony very quickly. They have the ability to nest in very unlikely places.

WHAT THEY LOOK LIKE

The Africanized honey bee is the same species as the European honey bee, so it's nearly identical to it. It takes an expert to tell the difference. Some of the measurements of Africanized bees are somewhat smaller than ordinary ones. Experts examine them under a microscope, and precise measurements are taken to determine what they are.

Because a casual eye examination can't tell the type of bee, you should stay away from all of them. Even regular European honey bees will become aggressive when disturbed.

KILLER BEE VENOM

An individual sting from an Africanized bee is no more dangerous than that of a domestic one. Where the danger lies is in the number of stings one will receive from them. They attack in greater numbers than domestic bees, and so the number of stings will be greater, up to ten times as many as from regular bees.

Allergies to bee stings are common and some are severe. In the worst cases, one sting may be fatal.

AVOIDING AFRICANIZED BEES

Avoiding Africanized bees is easier said than done. The best way is to be aware of where they have been known to nest. These places include trees and shrubs, wood piles, trash piles, flower pots, old tires, ground holes, chimneys, storage sheds, wall cavities, attics and crawl spaces, roof overhangs, eaves, water meter boxes, control valve boxes, evaporative coolers, mine shafts, and rock crevices.

These places cover a lot of territory, and it's hard to be watching all of them when you're out and about. You'll probably see some bees flying around before you are aware of the location of the nest. If you see bees flying around, it's best to stay away from that area. If you're out camping or hiking, be especially aware of them if you're near a water source. If they're in the area, they will most likely be seen around and on the water.

WHAT TO DO IN THE EVENT OF A BEE ATTACK

In the event of a bee attack, it's recommended by experts to cover your head and run. Especially cover your nose, mouth and eyes, even if you have to pull up your shirt to do this. The bees can sting through your shirt, so it isn't much protection anyway. Most healthy adults can outrun the bees, but they will pursue a long distance, up to a quarter of a mile.

Bees are attracted to the carbon dioxide that we breathe out and will target your nose and mouth first. Many people have died from asphyxiation from bees obstructing their airway. The Florida apiary chief states that more people die from asphyxiation than die from bee stings. Eyes are vulnerable also. It's imperative to cover your head.

If attacked while in the countryside or camping, head for the shelter of your vehicle or campsite where there may be a tent, blanket, or sleeping bag to get under. If you're at home, try to get to the house or other shelter.

Do not jump into water. The bees will wait until you resurface and continue their attack.

Do not swat at the bees or flail your arms. They are attracted by motion. Crushed bees emit a smell that will attract more of them.

Once you have reached safety, remove the stingers. When a honey bee stings, it leaves its stinger in the skin and dies. If the stingers are left in the skin, venom will continue to enter your body for a short time, so they must be removed. Don't use tweezers or your fingers to do this. This will squeeze the stinger and cause more venom to enter the wound. Scrape the stinger out sideways using your finger nail, the back of a knife blade, credit card or other similar object.

If you have been stung more than fifteen times or are feeling ill, seek medical attention at once. Some people are allergic to bees and don't realize it. You may need to be given something for pain and inflammation.

CONCLUSION

We hope that that this book has helped you to better understand our southwestern deserts and will help enable you to better live in, recreate on, and visit them in the safest and most enjoyable manner possible.

It's important to remember when you are outdoors anywhere, whether it's in our wonderful deserts or the beautiful wooded forests with lakes and creeks, that you need to be aware of the fact that everything there has its place in nature and is part of the environment. It's there because it belongs there and should remain undisturbed as much as possible. Understand this, learn to live with the land, not just on the land, and become part of the environment, not a stranger to it. Enjoy all it has to offer.

BIBLIOGRAPHY

"2011 Annual Report of ATV Related Deaths and Injuries."
cpsc.gov/search/researchandstatistics.

"Africanized Honey Bees."
en.wikipedia.org/wiki/Africanized_bee. Visited May 26, 2013.

Asmi.az.gov/abandonedmineseducation.asp. Visited July, 2011.

"Arizona Brown Spider." *ehow.com/info_8381613-spiders-southern-Arizona.html.*

"Arizona Coral Snake." *desert museum.org/books/nhsd_coral_snake.php.*

"Arizona 2013 Fact Sheet."
children'ssafetynetwork.org/states.state information.Arizona.

Azcentral.com/new/wildfires/yarnell.

"Arizona Rattlesnakes." *azgfd.gov/w_c/Arizona-rattlesnakes.shtml.*

Bartlett, Dick. "Coral Snakes."
reptile channel.com/authors/dickbartlett.

"Black Widow Spider."
schools-wikipedia.org/wp/b/black_widow_spider

"Black Widow Spider Bites."
desertusa.com/insects/blackwidowspiderbite.

"Black Widow Spider Bite."
emedicinehealth.com/black_widow_spider_bite.

"Black Widow Spider Bites."
desertusa.com/insects/black_widow_spider_bite.

"Black Widow Spiders in the Low Desert."
Ag.Arizona.edu/aricopa/garden/html/t-tips.

"Brown Spider." *desert museum.org/books/nhsd_brown_spider_php.*

Brown, Wizzie. ""Scorpions." *insects.tamu.edu.*

"Centipede Ecology." *en.wikipedia.org/wiki/centipede*

"Centipede Hazards to Humans."
en.wikipedia.org/wiki/centipede.

children'ssafetynetwork.org/states.state information.Arizona.

"Coral Snake."
encyclopedia.com/topic/coral_snake.

"Coral Snake Distribution." *en.wikipedia.org/wiki/coral_snake.*

Daisymountainfire.org/events/mine_shaft.PDF.

"Distribution of Africanized Honey Bees."
national atlas.gov >Map Layers.

Dreier, Hannah. "Officer Killed in Fall From Marked Area of Mount Charleston Near Las Vegas."
therepublic.com/usrescuerkilled.

forest fire.nau.edu/statistics.htminclweb.org/stats/3

Geeky Melanie. "Death by Cactus." *twosexygeeks.com/10deathsthataresobizzaretheyarenearlyfuny.*

"Get Rid of Black Widow Spiders." *doyourownpestcontrol.com/black-widow-spiders-c-310.html?source=search_page-category_box.*

"Gila Monster-Arizona." *Arizona leisure.com/Gila monster-html.*

"Gila Monster." *en.wikipedia.org/wiki/gila_monster.*

"Gila Monster." *national zoo.si.edu/.../Facts/FactSheets/Gilamonster.cfm.*

"Guns Blamed for Sparking Some Wildfires in West." *cbsnews.com/8301-20/_162-57466270.*

Hedding, Judy. "Black Widow Spiders." *Phoenix.about.com/cs/desert/a/spider/htm.*

Hedding, Judy. "Killer Bees." *Phoenix.about.com/cs/desert/a/killerbees01_2.htm.*

Hedding, Judy. "Scorpions in Phoenix." *phoenix.about.com/od/scorpions/tp/scorpionsinphoenix.htm.*

"How the African Honey Bee Differs From the European Honey Bee." *ars.usda.gov/Research/docs.htm?docid=11.*

Ivanyi, Craig. "Rattlesnakes." *desert museum.org/books/nhsd.rattlesnakes.html?print=y.*

"Killer Bees."

desertusa.com/mag98/sep/stories/kbees.htm.

Kinsey, Beth. "Arizona Brown Spider." *firefly forest.net/Arizona-spiders-and-arachnids.*

Kinsey, Beth. "Arizona Giant Centipede." *firefly forest.net/firefly/2008/09/05/Arizona-giant-centipede.*

Lizotte, Renee. "Centipedes and Millipedes" *desertmuseum.org/books/nhsd_centipede.php?print=y.*

"New Heat Study." *direct log.health.azdhs.gov/tag=heat-exposure.*

Prchal, Stephan L. "Scorpions." *desert museum.org/books/nhsd_scorpions.new.html.*

"Rattlesnakes." *desertusa.com/reptiles/rattlesnakes.html.*

"Rodeo Chediski Fire." *Wikipedia.org/wiki/rodeo.*

Schmidt, Justin O. "Wasps." *desertusa.org/books/nhsd_wasps.php?print=y.*

Sky News Team. "Las Vegas Policeman Killed in Helicopter Fall." *news.sky.com/119374.*

"Tarantula." *en.wikipedia.org/wiki/tarantula.*

"Tarantula." *desertmuseum.org/books/nhsd_tarantula.php.*

"Tarantula Hawk Behavior." *en.wikipedia.org/wiki/Tarantula_hawk#Behavior.*

"The Arizona Giant Centipede." *bugguide.net/node/view 20/centipedes.*

"The Coral Snake." *wfinet/coralsnake .thesmokingun.com.documents/arizonaforestfire-879543 usa.gov/cpscpuls/prerel/primt/12/12209.html.*

"What to do if Attacked by Africanized Honey Bees."
ars.usda.gov/Research/docs.htm?docid=11059&page=3.

Zmuida, China. "Desert Spiders in Arizona."
ehow.com>Health>Public Health & Safety>Outdoor Safety.

Made in the USA
Lexington, KY
12 February 2018